# It Will Be
# *Worth It All*

LINDA SKELTON

First Printing

Published by
Southern Lion Books
Historical Publications
1070 Jordan Road
Madison, GA 30650

www.southernlionbooks.com

Manufactured in the United States of America.

ISBN-13: 9781935272243


Library of Congress Control Number: 2015933654

The paper in this book meets the guidelines for permanence and durability of the Committee on Production Guidelines for Book Longevity of the Council on Library Resources.


Cover Design by Natalie's Awesome

# Foreword

We are honored to have been asked to write the fore-word for this inspiring book. We pray that God will use it for His glory as He used the Skeltons during their 35 years in the Ivory Coast.

The Skeltons have been our best friends for almost 40 years and we have many memories of shared family vacations and gatherings. Our children grew up together and remain friends to this day. Knowing the Skeltons and experiencing life with them has been an exciting adventure! We have lived through many of the events in this book. We have shared many happy as well as sad times with them. Some of what is in this book may seem unbelievable, miraculous in fact, and they are because they were miracles that God accomplished through them. God allowed them to go through many crises to show His power and use them as an example to others.

The Lord worked through the Skeltons in a number of ways. They started a Bible school for pastors and trained church leaders. They started churches in Abidjan as well as the remote villages in the western part of the country. Their biggest burden and undertaking at this time is the building of an orphanage in a village for 34 war orphans and widows. Even now, after Arnold's health forced him to return to the United States, they are still being used by God. We feel blessed to be a part of their lives.

Paula and Doug Simrell, MDiv, MRE
*Retired International Mission Board Missionaries*

# Contents

# Introduction

The Lord saved me when I was eleven years old. I remember being so convicted by the Holy Spirit that I would literally squeeze the pew in front of me during the church service to keep from running to the altar. I will never get over the joy and peace I had in knowing that I was born again! I have never doubted my conversion experience.

A year later, we had special revival meetings at our Southern Baptist Church in Covington, Georgia. The guest speaker was a missionary from Brazil. I had never seen a missionary before. We had prayed for several of them at the church but it meant absolutely nothing to me. I recall that the sermon wasn't anything spectacular but during the invitation, something happened in my heart which is as real today as it was then. That is why I love to speak in children's classes and groups! Who knows, there just may be a future foreign missionary sitting there before me.

Arnold Skelton and I met at Truett-McConnell College in Cleveland, Georgia. We began dating but it was a while before we shared our life's calling – to become a foreign missionary. He, also, had been called to the mission field during his teenage years. We both felt that the Lord had put us together and had a specific work for us to do. Arnold and I were married on July 15, 1967.

We lived in the Atlanta area for the next three years as we prepared to go to the Ivory Coast of French West Africa. Arnold continued to work with the State Highway Department and I was teaching kindergarten in our home church. In August of 1969, Arnold came home one day and said he had quit his job with the state and that we would now begin our deputation in different churches to get ready to leave for the mission field. We moved in with Arnold's parents and stayed there until our departure date on June 5, 1970. That was the day when we said our final goodbyes and boarded the plane to begin French language study in Paris, France.

At that time we had one child, Jason, who was only six weeks old. As the years passed, the Lord graciously blessed our home with four more children. Valerie was born in 1973 in Abidjan, Ivory Coast. John was born in 1976 at the same clinic as Valerie. Grady was born in 1979 at a Conservative Baptist Hospital in the small town of Ferkessedougou, Ivory Coast. Natalie was born in 1980 during our furlough and was only six weeks old when we returned to Africa. Our dear children have opened many doors to the hearts of Africans. The African people love them and have always been drawn to them.

I have been writing off and on for several years. I couldn't sleep at night because the burden to complete this book was weighing so strongly on my heart. So here is the story of our lives. While reading this book, you will most likely be laughing at one story and crying over the next one! I have tried to be as honest and open as I possibly could with my feelings and our experiences. One thing is for sure, you will certainly be amazed at the pathway the Lord has chosen for us to tread during these 35 years of serving Him in Africa.

I don't consider myself a writer, but I am convinced that the Lord wanted our life's story in print. If there is someone out there who gets closer to my Lord because of these writings or if there is someone who is called to serve the Lord on a foreign field after reading this book, then I will know that "It Will Be Worth It All!"

**Episode 1**

# Arnold's Personal Testimony

As I think and meditate, my mom, Johnnie Ethelene Griffin, always comes into my mind and heart! From my early childhood, when I was just a young, loud, energetic, little boy, Mom was sweet, gentle, but strict, as well! After all, World War II had just finished. Those were rough times for everyone living in those days.

Dad made it back from the Pacific front of the war without serious injuries. He was in the Navy serving his country as a real fighter on Iwo Jima, Japan. I am so proud of him and his service for our country!

As for my mom, she was raised a Wesleyan Methodist and came to know Jesus Christ as her Saviour in Billy Graham's "Atlanta-Cracker" Crusade in 1951. At that time, my mom started insisting that we children (my brother, sister, and I) regularly attend the First Methodist Church of Atlanta. Dr. Charles Allen was there at the church at that time. He was a great preacher and pastor who believed in missions, both home and abroad. Actually, I began to think about foreign mission work under his ministry and the prayers of my mom.

I was invited to spend the summer with my cousin, Larry Poole, and go to Vacation Bible School with him.

Needless to say, I was a stubborn 13-year-old. I politely told my Aunt Inez that I wasn't going to V.B.S. with my cousin! She quickly went to her garden where there were some large peach trees and picked off a big long branch! She proceeded to return to the house. She then stripped all the leaves from the branch in front of me and asked, "Arnold, you are going with your cousin, you hear?" I immediately responded, "Yes ma'am! I am going!" I obeyed, as told!

During the week at V.B.S., our teacher taught all about sin, the sacrifice for our sins, repentance and salvation that was personal. Wow! I was cut to the heart and received Jesus Christ as my Saviour at the end of the week. My uncle wasn't as excited as I was, but he said, "Oh, you will get over it!" I never did! Two weeks later, I began to hear God's call in my life. I thought I was going crazy! God spoke to my heart, especially at night. My mom prayed for me and she said that she knew God was going to send me to the mission field one day.

Well, that day did come after I fought His call for four more years! Finally, at the bottom of a 60 ft. cliff, after tumbling over and over five times into a ravine, I looked up into the night and said, "Lord, I'll go wherever you want me to go, do whatever you want me to do, learn whatever languages you want me to learn, and speak your message of Salvation to the lost!"

I announced my surrender to God's call in my home church, Macon Drive Baptist of Atlanta, Georgia, in the Atlanta Association of the Southern Baptist Convention. Everyone rejoiced in the church and my mom cried and cried! She said, "I knew He would call you and I knew you would finally surrender!" My dad thought I had lost my mind. The Lord told me to just be patient with him and he would come around to accept it.

I was counseled by my pastor, A.C. Carpenter, to go and "sharpen my axe in order to cut more wood." Our pastor recommended Truett-McConnell College in Cleveland, Georgia. It was in my sophomore year that God brought Linda and me together. After a lot of talking, praying, and waiting on God, we knew God wanted us to be life partners. We were married on July 15, 1967. What a life changer! God is so good and He knows exactly who He wants to serve Him and where for all their lives!

**Episode 2**

# Listen, He is calling

After speaking at a ladies' meeting in Atlanta, Georgia, I noticed that a well-dressed, elderly lady kept looking at me. When our eyes met, she began to speak her heart. She stated, "I hear what you are saying and what you have been through, but, honestly, you don't seem like the adventurous type to me!" My response, "Oh, I'm not, but my husband is the adventurous one. I just get behind him, close my eyes, hold on for dear life and off we go!" And that is the actual truth of the matter!

When I was a little girl, I wouldn't even sleep away from home. I always wanted to be in my own bed in the room next to my parents. If I had only known what the future held for me, I probably would have been horrified! I didn't know where the future would take me, but I am so glad that Jesus knew the path we would follow and He led us every step of the way. "Where He leads me, I will follow. I'll go with Him, with Him, all the way!"

A dear lady came to my house many years ago and this is her testimony. She said, "When I was a teenager, I knew beyond a shadow of a doubt that God had called me to be a foreign missionary. I lived out of His will, married out of His will, and must be the most miserable

4

person who ever lived. My whole life has counted for nothing. If only I could go back and start all over."

I have met many people with the same sad testimony. Our journey certainly hasn't been an easy one. The paths have often been steep and rocky but thanks to our Lord, He was always with us. I don't regret a single step of the way for I know with all certainty that it will be worth it all when we see Jesus. Now let's go back a few years!

**Episode 3**

# Hide and Seek

When I was two years old, my dad was throwing *Atlanta Journal and Constitution* newspapers from a bicycle every day. Several years passed and I will never forget the day my dad could finally buy a truck for his business. I have the black and white picture of the truck and my dad in it right beside me as I type! The first night, I invited the neighborhood children and their parents over to have a talent show in the back of the truck. All of us kids would take turns acting out skits or singing standing up on the truck. Those were the good old days when all the neighbors would bring a chair and would gather in someone's back yard just to have some fellowship. I miss those days!

I was probably one of the youngest children in the neighborhood. The older ones really didn't enjoy playing with me but I would bribe them into coming over. All I had to do was offer them some cookies or candy and I could usually have a friend to play with. Later on, my mom said she always felt sorry for me because I was always giving out all the goodies in the house just to be able to play with someone. I was the only child until I was seven years old.

I was used to getting all the attention so I wasn't too excited about sharing my life with a new baby sister. I

6

remember hearing Mama say what a terrible time she had trying to deliver me and it was even worse during the delivery of my sister seven years later. She had to make several trips to the hospital before Leta was born. I was out playing and a neighbor came by and asked me if my mom had the baby yet. I answered her by saying, "I don't know because she came back home a little while ago but now she has gone back to do it again!" Well, that was the perspective of a seven-year-old! I can also remember that every time I saw my dad go toward Leta, I would grab his hand and say, "Come on Daddy! Let's get out of here!"

It was a beautiful day and I had bribed the neighborhood kids into playing hide and seek with me. I was having so much fun! There were two concrete areas on each side of the front porch. I could hide there and go back and forth under the house. After a while, all the children were called home to eat their evening meal ("supper" as we called it)! I didn't know the game was over. I heard Mama and Daddy calling my name countless times but I was having so much fun moving around and hiding! I certainly didn't want to give up my spot! I did notice that the sun was rapidly setting but I just stayed quiet. I finally heard my parents say that it was time to call the police! That just didn't register with me and I can remember looking up as my parents climbed the front stairs to call and get help! I whispered, "Ssshhhhhh! Don't tell anyone where I am!" I got a scolding I will never forget!

## Episode 4

# The Goat Man

I am sure that many of you older readers have heard of the old bearded man who traveled all over the United States with his small carts and trailers and was accompanied by many goats. Therefore, everyone knew him as the Goat Man. These were the days before interstate highways so he was always off on some back road. Through the years, I remember my parents taking me to see him on several occasions and I was always amazed at the quantity of Bible verses he had written on everything! He would stand and talk about Jesus and the future gloom and doom of the entire world!

I was on a bus one day traveling from Conyers to Covington, Georgia. It was always a thrill to go to my grandmother's house by bus. As we approached a crowd of people who were gathered on the side of the road, I happened to see my dad out in the crowd looking and listening to the Goat Man. At that time, my dad sold Coastal States Life Insurance and did a good bit of traveling around. I jumped up in the bus and shouted, "Can you please let me off? There is my dad!" Everyone in the bus looked at me and they all asked the same question at the same time. "Is the Goat Man your dad?" After that day, every time someone mentioned the Goat Man, my dad's shoulders would literally shake with laughter!

**Episode 5**

# Stranger in Our Home

It was a beautiful fall day. I was 16 years old and was out riding in the car with my little sister and an older friend of mine. My parents were at work. They had a clothing store in Conyers, Georgia. All of a sudden, we passed an old bent over man with a long white beard. He had a sack on his back. We first joked around and said it could be Santa Claus and then we became convinced that this was an angel and we should pick him up! The old man's eyes lit up as we stopped and asked him to get in the car and go home with us. We wanted to cook him some food to eat. (I know that you readers are about to gasp for air about now.) I realize it was dangerous and I certainly pray that my grandchildren never do anything like this!

I will never forget the peaceful look on his face as he sat at our dining room table and ate the eggs and bacon that we had prepared for him. The moment was broken as our phone rang. I thought Mama and Daddy would be proud of me for doing such a good deed. They always helped people in need! Mama asked what we were doing. I told her that we had the sweetest little old man sitting at our table eating. I heard her scream out and then she told me that Daddy was on his way home. That really scared me so we quickly escorted the man out to the car and took him back to the place where we had picked him up. By the time we got home, a horrified dad was standing in the back yard! We were severely scolded as to the danger of doing that.

We never saw the old man again, but till this day, I can close my eyes and see him sitting at our table with such a look of contentment. I didn't know the verse that says, "Be not forgetful to entertain strangers: for thereby some have entertained angels unawares." (Hebrews 13:2) I have no idea as to whom or what he was. What do you think?

**Episode 6**

# A Tragic Ending To A Tragic Life

My parents owned a small ladies' clothing store in Covington, Georgia. Often after high school, I would take the school bus to the store and stay until Mama was ready to go home.

I had often seen the little blonde, six-year-old girl come in the store to look around and talk to my parents. We were concerned that she just roamed the neighborhood with no supervision whatsoever. She wore dirty clothing every day and I never saw her when her hair was clean or even brushed.

It was approaching Easter and my parents had gotten in some beautiful dresses for little girls. Ruthie came in one day and immediately pointed to a pink lace dress. She proudly stated that her mother was going to come in and buy the dress for her to wear on Easter. After a couple of days passed, I remember my mother telling me that she had already decided to give the dress to Ruthie for Easter and she knew that Ruthie's mother had no intention of buying anything for her daughter.

As I was out one afternoon riding around with a friend, we approached a small bridge and it was covered with police cars, a fire truck, and an ambulance. I asked

11

a policeman what had happened and he told me a small girl had drowned in the river below. I had a terribly sick feeling in my stomach as I ran down the hill and that is when I saw something I will never forget as long as I live. The first scene I saw was Ruthie's blonde hair, twisted with a branch in it, as they pulled her from the water. I turned away in horror!

Ruthie finally got the dress of her dreams! She was buried in the pink dress covered in lace. I will always remember the poor little girl who roamed endlessly and had no one who even cared!

**Episode 7**

# Death in the Swamps!

During the Christmas holidays, Arnold visited his best friend, Pascal Garcia, who had moved with his family from Atlanta, Georgia to Denham Springs, Louisiana several years earlier. Pascal was home on leave from boot camp in the U. S. Navy. Arnold's mother felt uneasy when he boarded the bus to Louisiana. Although Arnold was only 16 years old, it was clear to his mother that he was running from the call of God in his life. She wondered what it would take to make him surrender to that call.

Christmas Eve began as a warm, beautiful day. Arnold, Pascal, and Kenneth (Pascal's younger brother) were in adventuresome spirits and decided to hike in the swamps where the Comite and Amite Rivers join. The boys left the Garcia home in short sleeves with only one sweater between them. All day long they hiked and talked of old times. It was great to be together again!

The time passed quickly and before the boys knew it, the sun was going down. It was time to start home. Fun turned to panic, and panic turned to horror as they realized that they were lost. To make matters worse, the temperature had begun to drop. The boys walked around the two rivers trying to find a way out, but it was to no avail. Completely exhausted and filled with fear, the boys

13

realized that if help didn't come soon, their young lives would be ended.

As temperatures plunged below freezing, the boys tried to build a fire to warm themselves. The fire wouldn't stay lit because of the dampness of the rivers and the freezing temperatures. They finally took their shoes off and put their feet in the ashes, but even that didn't help. Arnold didn't know it at the time but frostbite had already begun in his toes.

The three terrified teenagers decided that they should draw straws, and the one drawing the longest straw would go for help. They prayed together and then drew straws. Arnold drew the longest one. The boys made a raft by tying swamp trees together with vines. It was about midnight when they finished. Arnold slowly edged down into the icy water.

Suddenly, Pascal dove into the water and said, "I'm the oldest, I am trained for this so I'm going!" Pascal took his place on the raft and pushed off into the darkness. While they waited, Arnold and Kenneth prayed for Pascal's strength and safety and for themselves. Getting colder by the second, they jumped up and down to try to maintain some body heat.

After what seemed like an eternity, they heard Pascal's yell from the other side of the river. "I'm on the other side, and I'm going for help!" Arnold and Kenneth breathed a sigh of relief. They prayed and hoped that help would come for them before it was too late.

As the night passed, the two remaining young men heard the continual sound of firecrackers. They wondered how people could be so happy and joyful on this night-mare Christmas Eve. Later on, they found out that it was gun shots trying to locate them in the swamps. There was so much underbrush that the boys had to climb up on a large log. They heard a rattlesnake over in the bushes!

As dawn approached, Kenneth and Arnold could hear the rumbling of a nearby tractor. They screamed and yelled for help until they were hoarse. A farmer plowing his land couldn't figure out why his dogs were barking so loudly and wildly. He decided to get into his boat and go up the river to check things out. Seeing the boat coming towards them, they were both so relieved! The man picked them up and returned them to the Garcia home where they were immediately put into tubs of hot water to thaw their bodies. Police and media were everywhere! A doctor was called to examine them. Arnold kept asking, "Where is Pascal?"

They were told how Pascal had reached the other side of the river. Tired and cold from the freezing water and temperature, he sat on a log, removed his boots, and began rubbing his feet. Pascal was found in a sitting position on the log – frozen to death!

On the day of Pascal's funeral, Arnold approached the casket and looked into his best friend's cold and lifeless face. Arnold felt he was the one who should have died instead of Pascal. God had His hand on Arnold. He was calling him to go and preach on a foreign field. Arnold would continue to run from the Lord, just like Jonah, the prophet and preacher, before his complete surrender.

**Episode 8**

# Surrender at the Bottom of a Cliff

Arnold had graduated from high school. He thought he had it made in life. He had a good job, making lots of money, and was driving a brand new Volkswagen. He didn't know Romans 11:29, "For the gifts and calling of God are without repentance." Although Arnold had stared death in the face four times already, he still refused to surrender himself to the Lord.

Tommy, his first cousin, came to Atlanta to visit him. After a fun-packed weekend, Arnold drove Tommy back to Gillsville, Georgia. As they traveled the winding, curvy roads, it began drizzling rain. As Arnold and Tommy approached a sharp curve in the Oconee River Valley, they were temporarily blinded by the lights of an oncoming car. Arnold lost control of his Volkswagen and began sliding on the slick pavement. The next few seconds were a blur to them. The car left the road and tumbled over and over and over. It came to rest upside down at the bottom of a 60-foot cliff. The boys' first thought was that they were dead. Then reality came. They both had hunks of glass in their mouths, noses, and ears. Their faces and bodies were covered with small cuts from the broken glass. Arnold's head hit the rear-view mirror and the seats were torn from their rails. The small Volkswagen was crushed, but in spite of this, neither of them had one cut large enough to require stitches. They kicked open the doors and climbed out of the car. The two cousins groped around in the darkness trying to grab limbs and vines to be able to climb up to the top of the ravine. Dazed, bloody, and exhausted, Arnold and Tommy made their way to their uncle's house only a mile away.

Only God knew that complete surrender to His will had taken place at the bottom of that cliff. Arnold, looking up into that black sky, had made a promise to God that he would keep for the rest of his life. "Lord, I will go where you want me to go; I will say what you want me to say; I will do what you want me to do."

## Episode 9

# A Hard Fish to Catch!

The first time I saw Arnold, he was preaching to the student body of Truett-McConnell College, where we both attended. I leaned over to the sophomore girl in front of me and asked if she knew who he was and if he was married! She told me his name, but laughed and said that if I was interested in him to forget it, as Arnold Skelton only thought about Jesus! Boy, did the wheels begin to turn in my head!

I had seen Arnold around campus many times. He was active in several groups and was even president of the Torchbearer's Club. This club had ministries in the jail and also in the nursing homes in Cleveland, Georgia. He always seemed to be in a hurry, so he didn't even notice the 18-year-old freshman who was scheming to meet him and get acquainted.

I joined the Torchbearer's Club and was ridiculously faithful to all the meetings! I would usually be there before any of the others arrived. The president finally noticed me and even asked my best friend where I was when I was sick and missed one of the weekly meetings. I was at least on the right trail!

One day my roommates and I decided to speed this romance up a little bit. Arnold always stood outside the bus until it was completely full of students going to church on Wednesday nights. There was a church out in the country and there was another church in the city. We knew Arnold always got on last and sat on the front row of the bus. My roommates made sure that I was sitting next to Arnold on that trip. He sat down next to me and my heart was beating so fast! Surely he could hear it! He asked me which church I was going to that night and when I replied that I was going to the country church, he said, "Oh, good!" I just knew he was going to sit with me at church! When we arrived at the city church, Arnold jumped up and said, "See you later!" My heart sank to my feet! I decided to leave this romance with the Lord, and sure enough, things began to change!

Two months later, we began dating and before long we were planning our future. What a wonderful day when we both shared our desire and calling of God to be missionaries. This special confirmation from God, which showed us that we were in His complete and perfect will, strengthened our love for Him and for each other. Forward! March!

We were married on July 15, 1967. Life wasn't easy, and it was rare when we had time alone together. Arnold worked all day, five days a week, and went to Bible School until 10:30 three nights a week. There were always church meetings to attend on the other nights.

We had an average of five dollars a week to spend for groceries. Our main diet consisted of dried beans, polk salad, that Arnold picked while on his job with the State Highway Department, and fried chicken gizzards. One night I decided to drink some grape juice with our nightly feast! The combination was not a wise choice. I thought I would actually die before morning came! Till this day, I have never eaten another bite of polk salad! I am sure that a lot of our readers are familiar with the popular 1969 song, "Polk Salad Annie" by Tony Joe White. The last line of the song says it all! "Carry it home and cook it for supper 'cause that's about all they had to eat, but they did alright!" Guess Arnold and I did alright, too!

To enhance the menu a bit, a friend and I decided to put food coloring on cornbread and deviled eggs. The food tasted the same as it always did, so we were shocked and surprised when our husbands couldn't eat that night and pushed their plates away. I can't imagine green cornbread and blue deviled eggs taking away one's appetite!

Arnold and I picked up empty Coke bottles on the side of the road to sell for gas money for our Volkswagen. But we were happy, and we look back at those days with fond, loving memories, realizing that God was preparing us for the experiences and the miles we would travel together in our future in Africa.

Preparing to go to Africa dominated our every thought and decision. Even though I knew beyond a shadow of a doubt that God had called me, I was afraid of that final step – our departure. Time passed quickly and then it was official, we were going to Africa! I had always been extremely close to my parents and my only sister. I had always lived near them, and I knew they were there when I needed them. Was it really possible that I would soon be boarding a huge airplane that would take me across the Atlantic Ocean away from them? The only vision I could muster in my mind about Africa was taken from the Tarzan movies! Plus, I had never flown before!

As I began to think back over my childhood days and started to dread the good-byes to friends and family, I asked the Lord to help me. I asked Him to give me the peace, joy, and victory in trusting Him that I so desperately needed. The Lord gave me the verse, Joshua 1:9, "Have not I commanded thee? Be strong and of a good courage; be not afraid, neither be thou dismayed: for the Lord thy God is with thee whithersoever thou goest." This has become my life's verse.

On June 5, 1970, Arnold, Jason, who was then six weeks old, and I hugged our precious families for the last time for four years. As the plane left Atlanta and the familiar faces that we loved, I kept repeating my special verse from the Lord. We had no idea what the Lord had in store for our lives but we were willing and ready to follow Him!

## Episode 10

# Moving On

I can vividly remember my mother telling me that she felt sorry for me! She said that I would get something for a year or so and then have to give it up to move to another place. I thought a minute and told her that I felt sorry for her because she had to keep the same old things all her life. Yes, moving from place to place has been our way of life for all these many years. I guess it really started when we were married on July 15, 1967. Let's go back a few years!

Our first little home was a literal nightmare! After our two day honeymoon in North Georgia, we moved into our little dump. It was moldy and smelled horrible. It had one open room and a small kitchen. This first place was actually the basement apartment of an elderly woman. It was depressing living there, to say the least, but I guess I didn't mind too much because I had finally become Mrs. Arnold Skelton! I remember that Arnold's 15-year-old sister came over to spend the night with us during those days, and she slept in the bed with us because she was afraid of creepy things crawling around. I had the same feelings!

All this time as we were preparing to go to Africa, Arnold was working with the State Highway Department. An older preacher and his wife offered us another place to live in their unfinished basement. This apartment was even worse than the first one had been! It had a dirt floor in the corner that was supposed to have been a bathroom sooner or later. Yes, you are right! It must have been later because the couple never did anything to that apartment. It was very inconvenient for us to have to climb the stairs each time to share the bathroom with that elderly couple. I remember the first time my mother came to visit she had to pull over to the side of the road on the way home because she was crying so hard! She couldn't even see the road!

That apartment was crawling with roaches! When we would come home and go down the stairs, I would have the bug spray in my hand and as soon as the light was on, I would start pumping the spray and screaming at the same time. Those roaches would run across our kitchen table, fall, hit the floor and keep on trucking! One day I came down the stairs to see Arnold sitting in a chair reading a book. A huge rat about half the size of a possum was directly behind Arnold in the screen-less window! I let out a blood curdling scream! Could this have been preparing me for the years I spent in Africa? At least we had screens on our windows in the Ivory Coast, that we always put on ourselves, before we moved in a house!

The icing on the cake was when we were asleep one night in that same apartment and I felt something up on my chest. It was a stray cat from the neighborhood that had jumped in the window, climbed up on our bed, mounted my chest, and was now looking into my eyes! I screamed so loudly that the poor frightened preacher upstairs came running down to our apartment wearing only his boxer shorts! To make matters much worse, he was standing at the foot of our bed with a shotgun pointing at us! He thought a burglar had come in!

I was so discouraged because Arnold was never home. He worked all day, came home to shower and eat dinner, Bible school three nights a week, and different church meetings and street preaching the other nights. I spent way too much time alone in that house of horrors!

One day, Arnold came home and told me to get in the car because he wanted to show me something. He drove to the cutest little dollhouse I had ever seen. I asked him who lived there and he responded, "Mr. and Mrs. Arnold Skelton!" We were so happy there! I walked across the field each morning to Macon Drive Baptist Church in Lakewood, Georgia where I taught kindergarten. We lived in the dollhouse until Arnold came in one day and told me he had quit his job. It was time to make concrete plans to leave the only country we had ever known!

The next months were busy going to different churches to raise financial support before our departure. We were finally making definite plans to leave the country and go to Africa! We moved in with Arnold's parents for about eight months until our first son, Jason, was born. Six weeks later, I was boarding an airplane for the very first time in my life to follow our dreams and our calling. There were so many new and different things ahead of us. I was a new mother, first time traveler, first time ever leaving my family, new language and new customs! I should have realized that the Lord had our life's purpose all planned out and waiting for us to follow! I am so glad we did!

**Episode 11**

# Provisions of God

Our courtship and marriage were founded on faith in the Lord to provide for us and our needs, no matter how large or small they might be. Growing up, I always had everything I needed and more, so this kind of lifestyle was alien to me. Nevertheless, I was more than willing to test the promises of God and see if they were all true.

In the early days, it's a wonder we didn't cause our parents to go into cardiac arrest because of our antics. We were very zealous for the Lord, but I must admit we were without wisdom in a lot of situations.

Each Friday night, Arnold and several young preacher boys would go to downtown Atlanta and preach on the streets in the area of a large park. When Arnold walked out the door each week, I never knew who he would bring home with him!

One Friday night after the street service, Arnold showed up at our house bringing home two houseguests! He had found a young married couple sleeping under the park benches or any other place they could find. They heard the Gospel and had accepted the Lord into their lives that night. Their earlier lives were filled with drugs, stealing, prostitution, and suspicion of everyone they met. I must admit I was very leery of this man and woman as Arnold led them into our house and gave them our bed. At this time, we were still living in the unfinished basement of an elderly couple. Arnold and I managed to get through the night on the sofa in the living room. They stayed with us for a couple of days, and then the people at our church helped us get them a small bedroom apartment up the road from us. The man got a job and I was amazed at the change in their lifestyle. At almost every service, one or the other would stand up and give glory to God for saving them and giving them a reason to live. We went to the mission field shortly after that and they later moved to the other side of Atlanta. We lost contact with them but we pray that Jesus is still first in their lives no matter where they are. Yes, it was dangerous having them in our home, but we did what we could and what we thought was right at the time.

Another time, Arnold brought a huge man from the streets home with him. He had just been released from prison on a charge of assisting in a murder! I did put my foot down that time and told Arnold that he could stay with the visitor but I wasn't staying. So Arnold took him to the church and stayed with him all night while I stayed home. The next day, Arnold took the man to a mission where he could stay and eat in downtown Atlanta.

The angriest I ever became with Arnold was the time I was preparing dinner and asked him to go to the store at the corner and buy some bread. He left the house immediately but stayed gone for more than an hour. I was worried sick thinking he had been in an automobile accident. He finally came home all excited about a man he had been witnessing to. That was fine, but where was the bread? In his excitement, Arnold had forgotten to buy the bread! I bit my tongue and asked him to please go back and get the bread. Enough is enough! Right? He apologized and left again, only to stay at the store for another hour. He came in red-faced and said he had forgotten the bread again, but he had brought the man home to stay with us for a few days. At least we wouldn't have to move to the sofa this time because now we had an extra bedroom in our rented and furnished apartment. This man had been wandering from place to place and hadn't been in a tub or shower for days and days. Just looking at the grime and filth on him made me very nervous! We didn't have a shower, so he stayed in the bathtub for a couple of hours. When he finally came out, it looked like someone had bathed a big, hairy, muddy dog in our bathroom! Our guest stayed with us for about a week, and I must admit, I was very nervous the whole time. We never saw him after he left. I sincerely hope and pray that he is somewhere in service for the Lord.

During this time, Arnold and I were having a difficult time financially. One night he came home from work and there was no food in the house. It was a Wednesday night, so we went on to prayer meeting, but with empty stomachs. We didn't tell one person about our situation. After church, we drove home to our apartment. As we arrived, we saw three large sacks of groceries sitting at our front door! There wasn't a note or a clue as to who sent them, but there was enough food inside those sacks to last us for two weeks! We were just beginning to see God's provision in our lives in a way that we never dreamed possible.

Once, when we were home on furlough and getting ready to go back to Africa, Arnold received a phone call from Colorado. He was invited to go out there and preach. Our family was earnestly praying about a four-wheel drive vehicle to take back to Africa for the bush ministry. We wanted a Jeep to reach the unreachable areas. Every day we prayed as a family for that great need. I can still hear our oldest son, Jason, as he always ended his prayers with this statement, "Lord, we don't see the Jeep, but we know it is coming!" That taught us a lot about praying with sincere expectation. Since that time, I have often ended my prayers with that powerful demonstration of real, child-like faith.

Arnold flew to Colorado and at the end of the first service, he was approached by a couple who desperately wanted him to stay in their home. Their son had been killed earlier on a mountain-climbing trip, and they were both shocked at the resemblance of Arnold to their son. He did go home with them and stayed in their son's room during the time in Colorado.

On the last night of the meeting, a man walked up to Arnold and told him that he had a used car lot and furthermore, the Lord had laid it on his heart to provide the vehicle needed for Africa. Arnold came back to Georgia, but in just a few days, he left for Colorado again, this time to drive our Jeep back to Atlanta. Here was a Christian businessman who listened to the prompting of the Holy Spirit and obeyed the Lord. It is strange, but the children didn't seem too surprised when I told them about the Jeep being provided. Lord, help me to trust you in complete faith and to believe with all my heart that even though I don't see it, I know it is coming!

Another time we were in a real predicament in Africa. I had always taught the children through correspondence courses, and they seemed to be happy. One day, Jason came to me and told me that he needed some friends and wanted so badly to go to the missionary boarding school that was about four hours from our home. I fully understood his need, but what I didn't understand was where we would possibly get the money to send him there and to buy all the clothes and supplies that he would need. We all began to pray. I registered Jason in the boarding school and began to plan for his entry in two months' time. I knew that if it was the Lord's will, the money would come, and we wouldn't have to sweat over it. A few days later, I received a letter from our dear friends from our college days. This couple had supported us for years and years, but it was rare that we heard from them in a personal letter. I trembled as I began to read. They had just sold their house for $50,000, and they felt led by the Lord to give us 10 percent of this amount for us to use in any way we wanted. Praise the Lord! That's the exact amount we needed! This wasn't accidental! Answers to prayers such as this one have done more to strengthen our family's faith in God than anything else. We do have a Saviour who cares about every detail in our lives!

Just a few months ago, we had written a letter asking our supporters to pray about the needed money for uniforms, books, soap, and other school supplies for our orphans in Yamoussoukro. The Lord graciously supplied, but afterwards, Coulibaly, our African director in charge of the orphans, wrote us and told us that in all the excitement about the supplies, he had forgotten to tell us about the $1,300.00 needed for their tuition. I told Arnold that there was no way that I could write another letter to our supporters. We decided to pray and keep it between the three of us! That is, Arnold, me, and the Lord! A few days later, a letter came from one of our supporting churches in North Carolina. The women at the church were in a meeting and one of the ladies spoke up and said that the Lord had put the Skelton's orphanage work on her heart and that she felt like they should take up an offering for our war orphans.

A few days later when I went down to the mailbox, there was a letter from the church. Inside there was a check for $1,295.00 to be used in any way needed for the orphans. I cried and praised the Lord all the way back to the house. I asked Arnold the question, "How much did Coulibaly say was needed for tuition?" I handed the check to Arnold and he also began crying and praising the Lord! Remember, we had decided not to mention this great need to anyone except Jesus! He is continuing to teach me that we must cast all our care on Him because He certainly cares for us!

**Episode 12**

# Near-Death Experience: "French Language School"

I often wonder why the Lord chose a timid, fearful, country girl who wouldn't even sleep away from her parents' home when she was a child, to go all the way to Africa. I had never been far from home with the exception of our Florida vacations each summer.

On that beautiful day in June, 1970, I said my final good-byes to parents, family, and friends to go to Paris, France, and begin the most difficult and discouraging time of my life. This is why I call this chapter my "near-death experience." I actually thought language school was going to kill me before it was over!

When we left, I had been a new mother for six weeks, and I had never changed a baby's diaper until Jason, our firstborn, came along. Horror of horrors, I stuck the diaper pin into his sensitive skin on my first diaper change! I ran crying to my mother and told her I thought I had brought him home from the hospital too soon.

Now, I can almost hear you saying how emotionally unstable you think I was during that time. You know what? You are right! I was a nervous wreck on the day we left. Although I had been preparing to go to the foreign mission field for the past eight years, I felt like backing out on the last day before our departure. To add to my deep distress, Jason had a severe case of diarrhea on the day we left.

The plane trip over the Atlantic was a nightmare for me. I was busy trying to keep Jason clean and changed, and I kept looking out the window to make sure that the wings were still attached! I searched the flight attendants' faces for any sign of distress caused by the plane's possible malfunction. Everyone looked relatively calm and pleasant so I tried to get some sleep, but to no avail. That is one trick that I have never mastered in all these years. I just cannot sleep on an airplane!

Veteran missionaries met us at the airport and took us to a hotel to spend the night until better arrangements could be made. Keep in mind that we were in a foreign country for the first time, all alone in a large hotel, and couldn't speak but one word of French. We were thankful for that one word but wondered why everyone looked at us like we were crazy. (We were saying "good day", and it was night time!)

The only restroom on our floor of the hotel was at the end of a very long hall. As I was trying to get out of the bathroom, a man walked in with only a towel around him! I almost fainted! I went running back to the room and found Arnold sitting on the side of the bed with his Bible in his hands. I took Jason in my arms. Arnold and I both began blubbering like two little lost kids.

Neither of us slept much that night. I lay there thinking about family back home and how far I was from all the familiar and comforting surroundings. I thought about our future and honestly wondered if the Lord really wanted this for our lives.

The veteran missionaries helped us find a very small, one-bedroom apartment. The landlords were an elderly couple and they seemed glad that we were living with them and helped us tremendously with our faltering French. I am positive that we provided many hours of entertainment and laughter for them as we tried to communicate in those early days!

We lived on the second floor and there were two other French couples who lived on the first and third floor. The main problem was that all six of us shared the same bathroom. Our infant son wore cloth diapers and there were many times that the bathroom was occupied or I didn't feel like going downstairs to dip his diapers in the toilet. That is when I would simply pile them out on the window ledge, and of course, they would freeze in the cold French weather! What a time I would have later on but we got through it!

Arnold and I roamed around the streets getting acquainted with the open-air markets and the new and strange language pouring out of everyone's mouth. We both did a lot of pointing at the food we wanted in the markets in those early days. It was like a continuous game of charades for us, except no one was laughing or having fun, and the game didn't seem to have an ending.

After about two months, we were settling down into a daily routine, and our understanding of the people and the language was improving. It was at this time we began language school. I left the house very early in the morning with another missionary lady. We walked several blocks, got on a train, rode about fifteen minutes, got on an underground metro for another fifteen or twenty minutes, and then walked another few blocks. All of this traveling was for a one-hour French class!

One day in class, the French teacher asked me to come to the front of the room and describe my small son to the class. I did not understand why the whole class burst into laughter when I told them how much I loved little Jason and that he was very enchanting. What I had actually said in French, to the international class in front of me, was that I kept my infant son in chains!

When I finally got home each day, Arnold turned the baby over to me. We quickly ate the lunch he had prepared, and then he left for school and followed the same paths and schedule as I had earlier. Arnold got home after dark each day, and then we had housework, baby care, and a whole lot of studying to do in the French language.

Arnold would often leave the house at night for an hour or so, and I wondered where in the world he was going. I later found out that he was out riding on his bicycle and crying! You see, we sometimes forget men have emotions, too. Arnold did not want to burden me with the ever-growing frustrations in his mind, but he was beginning to wonder if this really was God's call for our lives. Here we were in a strange land with a different language, different culture, and he was a new daddy! Had he made the right decision? Thank God we can look back today and say yes!

About seven months into language studies, I began a Bible club in an apartment area near our house. Surprisingly enough, there were several French children who came regularly to hear my strange accent. I felt like a little kid trying to communicate, even with children. In spite of my faltering French, the children came, and from time to time, some of the parents came, too. That is when I would really sweat! If they laughed at me, I never knew it. I'm sure they had fun in the evenings around the dinner table imitating that American trying to speak French!

In spite of the difficulty in learning a new language in a new culture with a new baby, the Lord blessed us, and we have some precious memories of our time there.

**Episode 13**

# Tea Party in the Desert

After our language study was completed, our mission board asked us to spend a few months in the Sahara Desert to translate the mission constitution into French, and to help the missionaries who were there to get registered with the government.

I was excited about finally arriving in Africa, but I wasn't prepared for what was ahead of us. Arnold and another missionary drove separate vehicles from Paris to a town in the middle of the Sahara Desert called Agadez, Niger. I felt an uneasiness in my heart that cold and dreary day as Arnold drove away with all our earthly belongings in and on top of the British Land Rover. They had a long and treacherous journey ahead of them. It took two weeks for them to reach their final destination. They had to cross the Mediterranean Sea on a huge barge on a rough, windy day. Arnold was so seasick he thought he would never see me again! He literally thought he was dying! He forced himself to write a farewell letter telling me he loved me and instructed the other missionary to give it to me at his death. The two men had received a great deal of information about traveling across the desert, but it didn't prepare them for their long and dangerous trip.

A couple of weeks later, Jason and I flew down from Paris and joined Arnold in Agadez. We shared the home of another missionary couple, Larry and Charlotte. The house was made of mud with wood shutters. The shutters did nothing to prevent the sand and dust from coming in the windows. Our water supply came from the oasis. Larry had a barrel on top of the house that he filled every two or three days. The water flowed into the kitchen from that barrel. There was an outside toilet! My, did we have some laughs out there! Roaches crawled everywhere! Charlotte and I both hated to walk out in the dark to that toilet, so we often walked out together and carried a flashlight that we held for each other. One night, Arnold and Larry were quite a distance away from home when they heard us laughing at the top of our lungs. One of them made the statement that Charlotte and Linda must be out at the toilet because they heard us laughing so loudly!

Before I go any further, I have to tell you that I am deathly afraid of mice. My friends all know that I had much rather meet up with a snake than a mouse. Laugh if you want to, but it is the truth! Much to my horror, my worst nightmare came true! That mud house was full of little jumping mice that we called "kangaroo mice." I picked up a folded washcloth one day and something moved inside. It was a mouse hiding between the folds. I never dreamed I could throw something so fast and so far! At night, Arnold would sit on the side of the bed and shoot mice with his pellet rifle as I stood on the bed and shook the curtain over the closet to force the little creatures out into the open! There was a continual fear that one or more of those mice would get up in the bed with us! I was always glad to see the morning sun come up!

We had a thatched roof on the mud house where we lived. There was a large bird nest right over our bed. Each morning the birds woke us up by flying down by our faces and chirping loudly! I have always loved birds but this was taking it a little too far!

We were honored one day when we received an invitation to drive out into the desert and visit with the nomadic people. When we arrived, all the women were sitting around in a large circle with their legs crossed. The men were doing likewise in an even larger circle just a few feet away. Jason and I were ushered to the middle of the ladies' circle where we sat down on the ground. I was comforted by the smiling and amused faces of the women. I glanced over my shoulder and saw that Arnold had taken his place in the middle of the men's circle.

They had prepared a thick and very strong tea to serve us. I was relieved when they began with Jason and I was second in drinking from the only glass they had. I prided myself on being able to adjust so well, when the small glass had gone all around the circle and everyone had drunk some of the tea. Boy, was I surprised when it was again my time to drink out of that same glass! It went around the circle two times. This "tea party" did more to help me adjust to different cultures and tribes than anything else could have. It prepared me for the years ahead when we would have to forget our American way of doing things and actually be a part of the dear people where God had called us to minister.

After several months, we again packed up all our earthly belongings in the Land Rover and were finally on our way to the land we had only dreamed and prayed about – the Ivory Coast of West Africa. Jason made the long trip to the Ivory Coast sitting between his daddy and me on his potty chair. Yes, he was totally potty-trained when we reached our destination two weeks later!

Our nightly shower was such a welcomed blessing. We drove all day long on the dusty roads. It was rare if we met another vehicle. Our meals consisted of grilled, peppered chicken, which the Africans cooked in their villages along the way. One night we were anxious to find a campsite and put up our tent. We decided to take the chicken with us and eat it just before we settled in for the night. We threw the bones outside near the tent, never thinking twice about it. We were so tired, we quickly went to sleep. Suddenly, a noise from outside the tent awakened us. Something was crunching those bones we had thrown out! Arnold motioned for me to be very quiet as he unzipped the tent and peeped out. We were surrounded by wild hyenas! We prayed, "Lord, please don't let Jason wake up and start crying!" After they gobbled up the bones, the pack of wild hyenas continued on into the night. We never threw bones or any type of food out on the ground in Africa again!

A couple of days later as we continued to travel, a large truck passed us and threw a rock into our windshield. We weren't able to see for all the broken glass, so we stopped and knocked the rest of the glass out. Later on that evening, we arrived in a small town and desperately tried to find someone who could put in a new windshield. We finally found an African who said he could help us, but we were forced to find a place to spend the night in that small town. Someone told us there were some Southern Baptist missionaries living there, but they weren't home when we went to their house. We then went to the door of some other missionaries who seemed reluctant to even let us in the door. I understood and I probably would have reacted in the same way if a family as dirty and dusty as we were had come up to our door late at night. We looked like a bunch of hippies! The couple told us we could sleep in their basement print shop. I put long pajamas on Jason, and the three of us settled down on the floor with only a few blankets to lie on. It was hot and stuffy and the mosquitoes were already swarming badly. I didn't close my eyes all night! I was too busy swatting mosquitoes away from Jason. The next morning, I counted over sixty bites all over his face, arms, and hands. Two weeks later, I learned that Jason had contracted malaria while sleeping on the floor of the print shop.

When we finally arrived in Abidjan, the capital city of the Ivory Coast, I began shedding tears of joy – it was so beautiful and green! After living in the Sahara Desert for several months and not seeing any greenery there at all, I thought I was in Heaven! Even after all these years, I'm still enchanted by all the magnificent shades of green that you see intertwined in the Ivory Coast.

We didn't know one person in all the country. We had nowhere to go and no one was there to meet us! After our arrival, we were told to go to a missionary's house in Abidjan, the capital city, where we would find shelter until we could find our own house to rent. We had a tiny room with only a bed in it. We couldn't even pass each other in the room without getting up on the bed! Nevertheless, we were thankful to have a place to lay our heads after so many days of traveling through the desert.

These dear missionaries were so gracious in allowing us to stay with them for a couple of weeks. It wasn't easy, but we were finally where God had called us to live and minister!

**Episode 14**

# Five Greasy Thieves

Arnold and I learned many valuable lessons during our first four-year term in the Ivory Coast. We didn't know one person in all the country that night when we arrived after having driven all the way from Agadez in the Sahara Desert. We didn't have anyone to give us advice or to warn us of certain dangers.

After a couple of weeks, we finally got settled into our house, but we had to learn some things the hard way. For example, we had no idea that thieves were lurking on every corner in the Ivory Coast.

We befriended a man and his wife from Canada who were traveling through the country, and we asked them to stay at our home that night. We had two small bedrooms, so we naturally let them stay in our bedroom, and we slept in the room with Jason. We fellowshipped with our friends but went to bed early. I was six months pregnant and the heat was almost unbearable for me. We locked the doors' standard locks and thought we would be safe.

About 2:00 a.m., our lady guest was awakened by a sound and drowsily looked toward the bedroom door. A large figure of a man stood looking into the room. Our

41

friends had closed their door before retiring for the night, but now it was open. She wondered why in the world Arnold was standing at the door staring in at them. She thought he probably needed something from the bedroom, but before she could ask him what he wanted, the figure disappeared into the bathroom. Whatever it was, she guessed it could wait until morning.

All I can remember are the screams of the African who arrived at our house early the next morning and found Arnold's pants lying in the yard by the gate. His empty wallet was also in the yard, along with his identification cards and papers.

Arnold jumped up when he heard the screams and frantically searched for his pants. He was forced to grab other clothes from the closet as he raced out through the living room. The front door was wide open. It was then that we realized we had uninvited guests! Our friends cringed when they realized that it hadn't been Arnold looking in on them in the middle of the night.

There were black grease marks on the walls where the thieves had felt their way around in every room. We were told by the police that thieves often greased their naked bodies before they came into a house. This method was for their protection to make sure that they could easily slip away if one tried to grab them.

I wondered how I had slept through all the commotion. I found out. The thieves had burned a powder outside our window and fanned it inside for us to inhale. This put us in a deep sleep as they searched our house. The thieves couldn't have known we had friends over for the night.

My purse was gone. Our radio, our tape recorder, both of our watches, our camera, and all of our money was gone. We were thankful to be alive and safe. Our friends didn't stay with us for another night. They were so shaken up that they slept in a motel.

The intruders were never caught, but we learned an important lesson that day. We went to great lengths to make sure we had plenty of deadbolt locks for the doors and even a dog or two in the yard. Most houses in the Ivory Coast have iron bars over the windows.

I've always heard that experience is the best teacher. I guess that's true. Even though some of our experiences have been very frightening, they have taught me that God is forever watching over us!

**Episode 15**

# Head On Collision!

Toward the end of our first term, on a Sunday morning, Arnold had gone to evangelize in a new area where we had been praying about starting another church. He had bought a Vespa scooter to travel around from one place to another.

Arnold had been gone for a couple of hours when a complete stranger knocked on my door. I was home alone with Jason, who was four years old, and Valerie, who was one-year-old. The African stranger had a look of horror on his face. He told me that he had seen my husband involved in a terrible traffic accident. A taxi had hit Arnold head-on! The collision threw Arnold up in the air and the witness told me that his helmet fell off and his head slammed up against the front window of the taxi. His next statement made me freeze with fear! "Someone took your husband to the clinic but I don't know where he was carried or how badly he was hurt. He was not moving when I saw him!"

I took the two children and stopped a taxi to go and find Arnold. My friend, another missionary, was at her mission church only a few miles away. I was completely composed until I walked inside the church and began explaining everything that I knew to my friend, Wilma. I just broke down! The only thing we could do was to go from one clinic to another until we found Arnold. We finally found him at the third clinic. His only injury after a collision like that was a fractured leg and the doctors were putting on a cast which covered his entire leg.

It was only a short time until our first furlough back to the States. We had been gone for four years and we were wondering how in the world Arnold could travel on the airplane with the cast on his leg. One night, Arnold asked me to pray that the Lord would heal his fractured leg. I prayed a one sentence prayer and the Lord answered! We had so much to do to get ready and move out of our rented house. The day before we traveled, against the doctors' orders, Arnold demanded that the cast be completely removed. The hospital staff reluctantly agreed and took it off. Arnold never had any more trouble with that leg. Faith or foolishness? You decide!

## Episode 16

# From Gangs to Glory

It has always been exciting to see how the Lord works, especially in the beginning of a new work. I get very sentimental when I remember the first church we started in the Ivory Coast.

The location was Sans-Fil. I was not prepared for what I saw. When we would drive into the area visiting the people or going to church, I would tell Jason, who was two years old, to keep his mouth closed so he wouldn't swallow the flies. The path toward the wooden church building seemed alive as it was lined with trash, slime, green water, and maggots. We balanced on narrow wooden boards as we made our way to the church building.

In fact, when our second child was born, I didn't take her to Sans-Fil for more than two months. I made all kinds of excuses. Finally, Arnold realized that I was simply avoiding taking our newborn daughter into that filth. So he began to do what he does best – preach to me! His words cut deeply as he told me that God had given Valerie to us and that if I continued to use her as an excuse, He could take her from us. So on the next Sunday, I prayerfully and fearfully packed her diaper bag and off we went! Upon our arrival, the church members came running out to the car to meet us. One of the men grabbed her first.

46

In their excitement, they were all trying to touch, kiss, and hold her at the same time. Was she smiling or did I just imagine that? The next scene will forever be in my mind. The African who had taken her from my arms was rubbing her gums with two of his fingers and talking about how soft she was!

I went home that day and built a small altar out of books in our bedroom and placed our tiny Valerie upon it. I knew the Lord had called us to serve there in the Ivory Coast. I knew that it was the Lord who had blessed our home with this precious little girl. I also realized that I had to turn over ALL my most precious possessions to Jesus to do a real and lasting work for Him. I was ready to do His will, no matter what the cost. So I gave Valerie to Him that Sunday afternoon in May of 1973. From that day until now, many years later, His blessings and watchful care have never ceased to amaze me.

We began our second church in Yopougon. It is now the home base for all the other ministries that the Lord has enabled us to establish in the Ivory Coast. In the beginning days, Arnold and I would leave the house in the early morning hours and drive to the open-air market. Arnold would climb on top of the Jeep to preach so the shoppers could see as well as hear him. We always traveled with a small, battery-operated microphone. I had a small accordion that I played to draw the attention of a crowd and believe me, it did just that! Why were these two crazy white people (or "peeled onions" as we are called by the Africans) putting on a performance right in the middle of an African market?

My talents in music are actually zero! I could scarcely play two songs on that accordion, but it didn't matter if I missed half of the notes because the Africans didn't know the songs or tunes anyway. In those early days, if the

Africans wanted to buy food from the market, they were forced to hear my accordion concert and Arnold's message from the Word of God. We had them trapped!

After we'd spent much time in prayer, along with running to and fro to get the needed paperwork, the Ivorian government accorded us a large piece of land right in the middle of a huge United Nations building project. The only stipulation was that a church building be constructed on the site.

In the middle of the church property, Arnold built a temporary shelter that had no sides, only a tin roof held up by wooden poles. Our pews consisted of 10 or 12 shaky benches without backs.

Of course, we were regarded with suspicion. Who or what had invaded that community? I can picture those early days so clearly. There was Arnold, Jason at four years of age, one-year-old Valerie, and me sitting out in the middle of a field trying to get some Africans to stop and at least talk to us. What a sight we were!

One morning a group of young men in the marketplace was shouting and making fun of Arnold and me. I was a little nervous, but as we finished the open-air meeting, Arnold made this announcement, "If any of you would like literature or someone to talk with, meet us at the church property up the street." Not a soul responded! We felt more than a little discouraged.

As we got ready to leave, a young man walked up on the property. We immediately recognized his face as one we'd seen in the crowd of mockers. He told us that his name was Maurice. He had been touched by the message and wanted to know more. Now, many years later, Maurice is still faithfully preaching the Word of God. He is now the assistant director of the national mission board and has supervised the opening of many new works in the western villages of the Ivory Coast. I am often reminded of the "patience" verse, Galatians 6:9, "And let us not be weary in well doing: for in due season we shall reap, if we faint not."

There was a gang in our neighborhood that was much feared. We knew Alain, the gang leader. He was very bold. He would let anyone know just how he felt about them or a particular situation without ever blinking an eye. Arnold and I both had tried to witness to him, but he wasn't interested in hearing about Jesus. He often threw rocks at the tin roof while I was trying to teach the children.

One day, just after Arnold had bought our "new" used car and left it parked behind the church, a young man came running in with startling news. Alain had done something terrible to our car. That was an understatement! The words, "Long live Satan" had been scratched in large letters on the hood of our car! It was so disheartening, to say the least. We could have reacted in several different ways. Personally, I wanted Arnold to punch the culprit in the nose and then call the police. Fortunately, Arnold didn't listen to me. He told me we just had to love this young man, forgive him, and pray for him. Arnold was right. I was wrong. We went on preaching the Gospel and claimed Ephesians 4:31 and 32, "Let all bitterness, and wrath, and anger, and clamor, and evil speaking, be put away from you, with all malice: And be ye kind one to another, tender-hearted, forgiving one another, even as God for Christ's sake hath forgiven you." Amen and, oh, me!

Not many months later, Alain, the gang leader appeared in church on Sunday and sat on the last bench. He continued to come and each service he moved up a few benches closer to Arnold.

My heart cried out in praise to Jesus when I saw his trembling body down at the altar. When he finished praying, he got up from that sacred place a new creature in Christ Jesus! "Therefore if any man be in Christ, he is a new creature: old things are passed away; behold, all things are become new" (2 Corinthians 5:17).

Have you been wrongfully hurt by a family member, a friend, a co-worker or even a brother or sister in the Lord? Patiently pray for that person and continue to show Christ's love through your life. Believe me, I know that this is the only way to be able to forgive. I am so thankful that Arnold didn't listen to me and punch Alain in the nose that day. He may have never come to Jesus!

**Episode 17**

# Monkey See, Monkey Do! #1

Maurice, our preacher out in the western side of the Ivory Coast, brought a girl chimpanzee to our house one day! I was excited, as I had never seen a real one! I didn't know just how smart or how strong they were! We named her Susie and made her a platform to sit and sleep on. We loved her more and more as the days passed!

Susie was extremely protective over Valerie. One day a little missionary girl was playing in the sand with Valerie, and Susie was sitting there enjoying the fun! She would mimic the girls by actually putting the sand in a small bucket, packing it down with her hands and then turning it upside down to make a little sand castle. If you gave her a knife and a piece of wood, she would sit there and whittle just like the children did! One day, the neighbor girl reached over and grabbed something out of Valerie's hand, and that is when Susie attacked her and bit her several times! It literally scared me to death! After that visit, we would always keep Susie away from the other children. She was so gentle with Valerie and Jason.

Our family was having dinner one night when we heard a scream from one of our African friends! He had come in the gate and saw that Susie had somehow slipped off the platform and hanged herself. We were all horrified! Her little body was still warm! This was our first chimpanzee and we all loved and enjoyed her so very much! It was like losing a family member! It would be a couple of years until Rosco came along.

**Episode 18**

# Monkey See, Monkey Do! #2

Arnold drove up to the gate and blew the horn so I could let him in our yard. At first glance, I thought he had a small African child in his lap in the car. When he stopped, I almost fainted! He had a baby chimpanzee hanging on around his neck for dear life! I was afraid to let him in the house, but Arnold reassured me that he was just a baby and wouldn't do any damage. Boy, did he eat those words!

The chimpanzee ran into our kitchen and jumped up on the cabinet where I had a large bunch of bananas. Rosco, as we later named him, started cramming several bananas into his mouth at one time and most of the bananas were coming out as the others were going in, and it was squashed all over the kitchen! Rosco then ran into the living room and began a wild climb up my curtains. By this time, I was shouting, "Somebody get him out of here!" There was a huge problem! He was so fast and so strong that we couldn't catch him! After pulling my curtains down to the floor, he did a mad dash back to the bedroom. He jumped up on our bed and began jumping and rolling around. Ok! Enough! We finally threw a quilt over him and actually tackled him. It was later that night when we got him settled in the huge tree out in our yard.

Rosco grew bigger and stronger as the days went by. He was so spoiled to his schedule. Every morning, he would scream until he got his cup of coffee with two teaspoons of sugar in it! Every afternoon, he had to have his cup of tea with two teaspoons of sugar in it! After drinking his beverages, he would run his fingers on the bottom of the cup and lick the sugar off of them.

There were little African boys riding around on bicycles selling popsicles they had made at their homes. They all had horns on the handle bars that they would blow to let the population know they were coming! When Rosco heard that horn, he went absolutely wild! He wouldn't stop screaming until we bought one and gave it to him. What a riot!

Rosco's favorite pastime was riding on the back of Jason's bicycle! He would sit there and hold on around Jason's waist. One day Rosco got loose and ran away. The people living around us were frightened as they saw the chimpanzee go running into a small store at the corner! Rosco began throwing cans around all over the place. It took quite a while to capture him and bring him back home!

The icing on the cake was when I heard our two-year-old daughter, Natalie, crying and I ran to the back yard. Rosco was holding her in one arm and was actually climbing up the tree with the other arm! I froze with fear! He went up to the top of the tree and I knew if he dropped her, it could kill her. I began trying to talk softly and coach Rosco down with my baby. It seemed like an eternity, but after a minute or so, he began the descent to the bottom of the tree still holding on to Natalie like she was his baby! After Rosco's feet touched the ground he held her for a moment longer in his arms and made a motion which looked like a kiss on her cheek and then dropped her on the ground. Whew! I ran and grabbed her, knowing we had to make some decisions about what to do with our ever-growing chimpanzee!

When I would go outside to feed Rosco, he would grab my hand and wouldn't let go. I was beginning to get afraid of what he could do! He was so much stronger than I was! We decided that we couldn't keep him any longer. There was a so-called zoo there in the capital city and they agreed to take Rosco. We went to see him a couple of times but he didn't seem to recognize us at all!

**Episode 19**

# Monkey See, Monkey Do! #3

One of our favorites was the little Guenon monkey that an African gave to John. We named her Zsa Zsa! Sometimes we would put diapers and baby clothes on her. She thought she was human because she actually slept in the bed with John. She would wrap herself around his waist and hold on to him all night long. Even when John would go to the restroom during the night, Zsa Zsa was there to accompany him! Sometimes Zsa Zsa would be out in the yard and when I would go out under the carport, she would always startle me by running and jumping on me!

We got a little white mouse during that time. I never thought I could love a mouse! There is just something about their tails! When I was shelling peas, the mouse would sit on its little pink hind legs and eat some peas. One day it was one of the children's birthday and there sat the little mouse up on the table enjoying a little birthday cake!

Zsa Zsa and the mouse developed a real friendship! Zsa Zsa would hold the little mouse and walk around with it. That was a sight to behold! We were so sad when one of the younger children accidentally squeezed the mouse too tightly one day. We never had another mouse after that!

**Episode 20**

# Move Over Cows. Here We Come!

After our first furlough, we had mixed emotions about flying to New York and climbing up on the huge freighter to go back to Africa. The "pro" to that means of travel was that we could put all our furniture and personal belongings on the freighter and then get them off immediately when we arrived in the Ivory Coast. Usually we sent our belongings on ahead of us in wooden crates or a rented container and it took weeks and even months to get them cleared with customs at the port. This was definitely a first for us!

My mother kept crying after she heard the word, "freighter." She was completely serious when she asked me if we would have to push the cows out of the way to have a place to sleep at night! Poor Mama! She had been watching too much television! In fact, the freighter's cabin had two passenger rooms and everything in it was stainless steel and spotless. We were the only passengers on the whole ship! Our small company consisted of Arnold, Jason, our five-year-old son, Valerie, our two-year-old daughter, and a huge Great Dane dog which had been given to us by a family member. I must admit that I was horrified that the children would fall overboard. I didn't let them get out of my sight, so needless to say, I was a nervous wreck!

57

The first two or three days were terrible for Arnold and me. I couldn't find my "sea legs" anywhere and I was also sick as a dog! Speaking of dogs, our Great Dane stayed out on the deck the whole trip and got fatter than a huge pig as he ate all the scraps from the meals served on the freighter. Arnold and I would lie on our beds and roll with the waves as we listened to the words of, "I Thank God for the Lighthouse" played on our small tape recorder. How I was longing to see a lighthouse to know we were near the shore. I was wondering when I would ever be able to stand up without going round and round!

When we had been on board two weeks, the freighter's captain informed us that we had to make a stop in Angola. No problem! Well, actually there was. War had just broken out in Angola, but we weren't aware of it. We were told that we would stay out at sea and not dock at the port at all. Arnold had this brainstorm! He would get off the freighter as we passed Monrovia, Liberia, and would get a bush taxi all the way to the Ivory Coast. He said he would then work on our car to get it running after a year of just sitting there in all that heat and he would also find us a house to rent. I didn't like the idea of being the only woman on the whole freighter but was willing to go along with him as it would be so wonderful having a house ready for us and being able to move in immediately.

I watched Arnold as he disappeared out in the Atlantic Ocean. Well, we were just going to sit in Angola and not have to leave the ship. How hard can that be? Two days later my little girl started screaming with an earache. It was bad so I asked the captain what we could do. There were no doctors on board so he said he would take us into the town and get some medical help. Her ear was bleeding by this time! I have never felt such fear as I did walking down the streets of Angola. There were huge tanks and trucks driving by very slowly and the soldiers all had machine guns pointing at us! I kept telling the children not to look at them, but they were innocent and thought it was exciting seeing all the guns! We got medical help, and just as the sun set that day, we were safe again in our rooms on the freighter.

Meantime, back to Arnold! Things didn't work out like we had expected. He arrived in the Ivory Coast and began working on our car when malaria hit him and hit him hard. He was out of his head with fever, chills, and vomiting. We were supposed to have arrived in the Ivory Coast after two weeks, but a whole month had passed since we stood on that deck of the freighter looking at the Statue of Liberty as we sailed past her. Our plans had drastically changed, so we had to work to get Arnold back on his feet and live in a mission house for a few more weeks until we could go looking for a house to rent.

**Episode 21**

# Meals from the Garbage Can

Returning to Africa after each furlough was quite an experience. Not only did we have to find a house to rent, but we also had the task of furnishing our new home. Most of our household belongings were sold or given away before we came back to America because we didn't have a place to store them during our year of furlough.

The most difficult time took place during our second term in Africa. We felt led to begin a work in a town called Abobo-Gare. We found a nice house by the market place, but the filthy conditions of this house were almost unbelievable. We learned that a family of fourteen people had moved out previously. From the looks of it, I thought there had been about 100 inhabitants!

I will never forget the day Arnold found that house. He took me to see it and I burst into tears. He kept telling me over and over to forget about the filth and focus on the possibility of the house. That was so hard to do, believe me! Later on, in other situations we encountered, I would remind myself of Arnold's words, "Overlook the filth and focus on the possibility."

Arnold worked on the outside while I tackled the inside. Our house was attached to another house on the back wall and on the other three sides were dirt roads. For days, Arnold had truckload after truckload of trash carried away. The biggest problem was that until we arrived, all the women in the neighborhood would throw their garbage and dirty water right in front of our house. In other words, we were moving into the community dump, and the smell proved it! Several African neighbors pitched in and helped, so it wasn't long until the slime, trash, and mosquito-breeding pools of dirty water were all cleaned up. At least we could drive up to our gate.

The bathroom was so filthy that I stood at the door and threw bottles of bleach all over the walls and floor. A hammer came in handy as I literally knocked the toilet seat off on the floor to keep from touching it! The kitchen cabinets had old papers and rotten food in them. As I opened them to desperately find some "possibilities," roaches crawled out. What a job ahead of us!

Several days later, I stood back and looked at the finished results. Amazing! I can truthfully say that after the cleaning, it turned out to be the nicest house we had ever lived in!

We became quite comfortable and were really getting things organized. We kept an old barrel out by the road where we put our trash each day. I was shocked one afternoon to see a teenage boy digging around in the trash can and gobbling garbage as savagely as a starving animal. I could tell he was not normal. He wore only a cloth around his waist and his movements reminded me of a wild, scared chimpanzee. Each time I tried to approach him, he ran off. The Lord prompted me with an idea. I began putting sandwiches, left-over biscuits, and fruit on top of the garbage can for him each evening. Before long, he knew where his dinner was coming from, so he would faithfully return to our house each day.

One day as I walked out, he saw me coming toward him. Instead of running, he just stood there and stared. I must admit that the look in his eyes frightened me. I walked back to our yard and motioned for him to join me. I picked up a basketball and began bouncing it. Suddenly, he ran up on the porch, grabbed the ball out of my hand, and began jumping around wildly, shrieking like a hyena! After a few minutes, he dropped the ball and went running up the street.

I never saw him again, but when I asked the neighbors about him, I found out that his parents chained him at night and let him roam in the daytime to find food to eat. They told everyone that he was demon-possessed, so they poisoned him, and he died shortly after.

During this incident, I was at home alone with my small children. I realize that, once again, God's protective hand was upon us, guarding us from harm.

I never found out if this boy was born in that condition or if something happened in his infancy. I often picture his face in my mind and remember that look in his eyes. It was the look of a scared and lost animal that had nowhere to go and no one who cared. This boy was shackled and bound in physical chains. As I think of him, I ask myself a question. In reality, was his condition any worse than those who say they know Jesus but who are still bound by sin and worldly gain? That's something to think about!

**Episode 22**

# Little Arnold, Miracle of God

As I had previously mentioned, Soye Maurice was one of our first converts when we began evangelizing in the area of Yopougon.

He and a group of his friends were standing around mocking and shouting as Arnold was standing up on top of our Land Rover preaching the Gospel at the open-air market. Arnold would try and be at the market preaching as soon as the sun came up every morning.

Although Maurice was taking part in the mocking, a work of God had begun in his heart that morning. After Arnold finished preaching, Maurice's friends dispersed, but Maurice was drawn by the Holy Spirit to follow Arnold back to our property (which would soon be our second and largest church to be built in the Ivory Coast). Maurice began asking questions and it wasn't long until he had accepted Jesus as his Saviour and would never be the same again!

Maurice came from a remote western village of the Ivory Coast and his burden was to return home and preach the Gospel to those who had never heard! It was just a few years after his conversion when he fell in love with a godly and precious lady, Angele, who came from a neighboring village. Oh, they were so sweet together! I can remember her shyness just being around us. She wouldn't even want to look at us in the eyes. If you saw her today you wouldn't know she was the same person. She, Maurice, and their five children have been like family members to us through the years.

Since Angele's first pregnancy was difficult from the beginning, Maurice wanted to send her to our house in the south of the Ivory Coast so that she would be near a doctor. We were so glad to have her and were all excited about having another little one in the family. The baby came earlier than expected and we were nervous as we drove Angele to the hospital. The nurses took Angele away and literally hours passed before we heard one word. Finally, someone came out and told us that they had done a C-section and that she was unconscious. They wouldn't let us see her. When we asked about the baby, no one seemed to know where the baby was! We searched everywhere and finally decided the baby hadn't survived and wondered what we would tell Maurice. He was out in the village and since the baby had come early, he had no idea what was going on! We had to send him a telegram to get in touch with him and let him know the devastating news.

Just when we were about to give up, one of the patients at the hospital told us that there was a newborn baby lying on a small cart down at the end of the hallway. We went running and there he was! We were so thankful that he was alive, but my heart broke as I picked him up in my arms. He was naked and hadn't been washed at all since birth. He was soaked with urine and feces. I asked the nurse what we should do and she said to take him home with us. Oh, my goodness! Angele is lying unconscious in the hospital. Maurice is still way out in the jungles of Africa, and here we are with a newborn baby that the parents have never even seen!

We took him home, and I was so nervous about him that we let him sleep in the middle of the big bed, and Valerie and I slept on the floor beside him. Two days later, the baby was burning up with a fever and his little neck and head were drawing backwards. We hurriedly returned to the hospital and found out that the baby had contracted spinal meningitis. They gave him injections, antibiotics and again, sent us home with the infant.

What a burden off of us when Maurice finally came down from the western side of the country and Angele was able to join the rest of us at our house. They named him Little Arnold and he is now a grown man, serving the Lord alongside of his dad in the western side of the Ivory Coast.

**Episode 23**

# Welcome Home, Daddy!

Arnold, Maurice, and another young preacher named Rene, had gone to some villages on the western side of the Ivory Coast to evangelize and preach the Gospel. Towards the evening, Arnold began having severe pain in his lower stomach. They had already walked from one of the villages to another so Arnold thought the pain was from walking so far through the jungle. He was sure he would feel better after resting for a while.

The pain worsened as the sun began to set. To make matters worse, heavy rains began falling on the jungle floors. After several hours of agonizing pain, Arnold realized that he must get medical help. By this time, he was throwing up and the pain had moved over to his right side. There was definitely a major problem. Arnold needed to get medical help, but he wasn't able to drive. Neither Maurice nor Rene knew how to drive. There was no choice in the matter! Arnold showed Maurice the gas pedal and the brake. There was no time for further driving lessons.

By the time they had traveled about one hour in the dark and wet night, Arnold began having convulsions. Somehow he managed to open the back door of the British Land Rover and fell out of the car into the mud.

Maurice and Rene thought the end had come for their missionary. Both men picked Arnold up and put him back into the vehicle. The nightmare continued. Approximately one and a half hours after leaving the village, the Land Rover came to a sudden halt. A huge tree had fallen over the road during the storm. There was absolutely no way to get around it. Time was precious, so they turned the vehicle around and drove back toward the village where they had begun the perilous trip. Three hours had passed, and they were back where they had started!

Maurice continued driving over the muddy roads, trying desperately to keep the Land Rover from falling into the potholes. Two hours later they arrived in a small town called Gagnoa and went directly to the Catholic hospital. There were no doctors on duty who could take care of Arnold so they were directed to a small bush clinic. An Ivorian surgeon was in charge and after a brief examination, they began preparing Arnold for an appendectomy.

Maurice was so terribly frightened that he left the clinic and traveled by bus to Abidjan to tell the children and me what had happened. He was so upset when he arrived at my door that all he could say was, "Papa was being rolled into an operating room and I don't know if he is dead or alive!" My heart dropped! A fellow missionary got on a bus that same day to go to Gagnoa and find Arnold. We were all amazed when we heard the following account.

There were two men hanging between life and death that needed immediate emergency appendectomies. The only means of sedating Arnold was to give him several huge gulps of homemade African palm whiskey to kill the pain. It must have done the job because Arnold didn't remember or feel a thing! Dr. Keita operated on the two men at the same time. The African died and Arnold lived!

The other missionary stayed for a week taking care of Arnold, preparing packages of chicken noodle soup on three stones in the open courtyard. Arnold had excellent care and felt privileged to have a stand-up electric fan blowing on him during those post-surgery days.

Back home in Abidjan, the children and I heard no news for another five or six days. We didn't have a telephone and telegrams took a long time to reach their destination. I have always held on to the old saying, "No news is good news." I knew that the missionary had found Arnold and that Arnold was being cared for. On the day that he could travel home, the children and I made a large banner to hang on the front of the garage. It said "Welcome Home Daddy," and my heart was saying, "Thank you, Jesus!"

**Episode 24**

# The Witchdoctor's Southern Accent

My husband's happiest times are when he is sharing the plan of salvation with lost Africans. The Lord has burdened our hearts for those far out in African villages who have never heard of the Bible, Jesus, or the "new birth" experience. When we go into a new village, we often hear the people refer to the Bible as the "Book of God." Our names have become "people of the Book." We love that title!

Arnold and two of the national preachers had prayed and decided to go to a new village called Maghaiho. The trip to the village took 14 hours by British Land Rover. Potholes in the dirt road were so deep and rough that the Land Rover would almost disappear as it went down into the holes.

The men were completely exhausted after their arrival that night. Arnold was led to a small mud hut with a palm-thatched roof. His bamboo bed was waiting for him in the corner. All it lacked was a sheet over it and a pillow (which he always takes with him when he travels).

The leaders of the village instructed Arnold to go to his hut and rest while the ladies prepared the evening meal. His rest started with a bang when a huge spider crawled up the wall by his bed. Keep in mind that Arnold has had encounters with bush rats weighing over 100 pounds, all kinds of snakes, starving hyenas, and other wild animals, but he will readily admit that his greatest fear is spiders. Thus, you can imagine his reaction as that huge, black, hairy creature crawled right up beside him. Knowing Arnold, I am sure it took quite a while for him to settle down after that episode!

It was very hot, humid, and stuffy inside the hut, so Arnold was lying on top of his sheet. He suddenly experienced an eerie and cold sensation. He felt as if a cool breeze was blowing through the hut. The large figure of a man appeared in the doorway. Arnold struggled to sit up and decide if this was an illusion or reality. The man in the doorway was all decked out in shells and skins hanging off his body. The moonlight shining behind him lit up his large frame which almost filled the doorway. Arnold thought it was one of the village men wanting something, so he asked the man what he needed. Arnold spoke to him in French. The uninvited guest began by saying that the white man and his book were not needed in that village. He told Arnold and his men to leave immediately or suffer the consequences. This type of confrontation had occurred more than a few times when Arnold had gone into villages for the first time. The amazing part of this story is that this African was not speaking his tribal language or French. He was speaking English with a southern accent! The Holy Spirit prompted Arnold to rebuke the witchdoctor in French. After the figure had run out the doorway, Arnold lay on his bamboo bed trying to sort out what had just taken place.

Raphael, the Christian who had invited Arnold to the village, came quickly when he saw the witchdoctor running away. He asked Arnold if the witchdoctor had hurt him. Arnold told Raphael that he was okay but wanted to find out who or what had been at his doorway. Raphael said the man was the village's most powerful witchdoctor, who was totally against the "white man's religion." Arnold asked Raphael where the man had learned English. "Oh," replied Raphael, "he doesn't know any languages except our own, and in all his life he has never left this area of three villages. He can't speak English!"

The meal the women prepared consisted of fluffy, steamed rice and a sauce made from a jungle animal. After the meal was over, the men prepared for the open-air meeting. There was a large crowd of villagers who sat all over the ground or on shaky, backless benches. The Christians began to sing and testify of the Lord's good-ness. A huge bonfire was blazing, and there were the sounds of drums beating in the air. Just before Arnold got up to preach in French (an interpreter translated Arnold's French into the tribal language), the witchdoctor, who had appeared in the doorway, came running into the service with arms spread open and began cursing the Christians and their God.

Arnold, Maurice (one of the other preachers), and Raphael fell on their faces and began to pray that Satan would be defeated and souls would be saved that very night. After a few minutes, the witchdoctor left, running out into the darkness of the jungle. Arnold didn't see him anymore and does not know what happened to him. Satan was defeated that night. In spite of Arnold's ex-treme fatigue, he felt totally revived when several vil-lagers began giving their hearts to Jesus.

Satan is always opposed to the salvation message being proclaimed. He will go to any extreme to hinder God's Word being preached, especially to those blinded by Satan who have never heard the good news of our Lord and Saviour.

## Episode 25

# Cerebral Malaria

After a two-week crusade in the village of Zou, Arnold returned home to Abidjan. This had been the beginning of our evangelism in the western villages of the Ivory Coast. He seemed extraordinarily tired, but I decided it was because of late nights of preaching and teaching and early mornings of prayer.

Three days after his return, while I was preparing breakfast, I went to check on Arnold. I couldn't wake him up. His eyes were rolling around in his head, and his body was rigid. We didn't have a telephone, so I screamed for our oldest son, Jason, to get our missionary friend to come help me. Jason was so afraid and upset that he didn't take time to put on his shoes. He ran barefoot through the market to get to the missionary's house.

Approximately 15 minutes passed before the two of them came running into the bedroom. We had to get emergency help quickly. We dragged Arnold out to the car and sat him up in the front seat. The car was small, and there was no way he could lie down. When we arrived at the French medical clinic, Arnold was examined by a doctor who told us that Arnold was semi-comatose. His body was rigid and he didn't seem to be conscious of his surroundings.

After tests, Arnold was diagnosed as having cerebral malaria. The prognosis wasn't at all encouraging. He stayed in the clinic for two weeks, in and out of consciousness. Some of our African friends stayed all night at the hospital and slept on the floor in the hallways just to be near Arnold and pray for him.

Family and friends in America begged us to come back to the States as soon as possible. The people at the airline told us that Arnold wouldn't be allowed to fly unless he was strong enough to walk out to the airplane unassisted.

We had no place to store our belongings while we went to the States, so as Arnold was convalescing at home, I began selling all our worldly possessions, one by one. I felt terrible the day I sold our bed and had to put my sick husband on the floor on a mattress!

Several missionaries told me that they were worried about me. They said that I was too calm during all of this. It was that wonderful provision and gift, called the Grace of God, that carried our family through the difficult times. Our daughter, Valerie, described it all too well. "Peace comes when the Grace of God "clicks" in!"

Arnold improved enough to make it up the airplane steps and we started our journey home. Later, he realized that he didn't remember anything about our departure. We had a layover of several hours in Madrid, Spain. Arnold stretched out on the airport chairs and slept until time to board our connecting flight.

We finally made it to Atlanta, and I was so relieved that we would be able to get the needed medical help from specialists. Our family had already made an appointment on the following morning for Arnold to have a complete physical examination by well-qualified doctors.

During our first night in Georgia, Arnold began having seizures, and his heart rate became very irregular. We called an ambulance, and he was soon admitted to the intensive care unit in an Atlanta hospital. Although I rode in the ambulance with Arnold, hospital personnel stopped me inside the emergency room. I kept shouting and repeating to the doctors that Arnold was allergic to penicillin and even a small amount could kill him. No one seemed to be listening. I was then ushered into a small room to fill out insurance forms. I was so upset that I actually couldn't think of my own name!

I finally walked out in the hallway and began crying in a corner of the emergency room. I felt arms slip around me, and an angelic voice asked, "Are you here alone?" I shook my head yes, and she answered, "Now you aren't alone. I am here with you." She just held me in her arms as I wept. A few minutes later, my mother-in-law arrived and I heard her say that she would stay with me. That stranger, that angel on earth, left me as quickly as she had appeared. I never saw her face, but I will never forget the compassion and love that lady showed to a complete stranger.

Arnold eventually recovered, but the doctors warned him not to return to Africa. That was many years ago. Just think what blessings and excitement we would have missed if we had listened to those doctors!

## Episode 26

# Poisoned, Yet Protected!

Living in the remote and faraway villages are many lost souls who have never seen a Bible or heard the sweet name of Jesus. We feel a great responsibility and desire to carry the Gospel to these precious people. Arnold usually took a trip out to the Southwest villages of the Ivory Coast every two months. He always traveled with at least two other Christian nationals.

The remote village of Zeregbo had been on our minds and hearts for a long time. The village chief had said that no white man would ever enter his village and leave it alive. Finally, after much prayer and fasting, Arnold and Maurice felt that it was definitely time to go into this village.

The African custom is to show hospitality to all guests who enter their village, even their enemies. The village people had heard that a white man was coming so they prepared a meal for him. As Arnold and Maurice entered the village, a young boy ran up and warned them not to eat or drink anything, as he had heard plans being made to poison the white man and his companion. After hearing this ominous news, Arnold looked at Maurice and said, "I am prepared to go in and eat whatever is set before us and so are you!" Maurice readily agreed.

Arnold and Maurice were ushered into a small mud hut where they were to partake of their meal. The villagers had prepared their normal red hot, pepper soup and monkey stew. After Arnold prayed over the food, he lifted the lid of the pot in front of them. A small monkey's hand came floating to the top of the stew! As Arnold was eating this monkey hand, which resembled that of a three or four month-old baby, he was thankful that the head of the monkey was given to Maurice to eat! After the two visitors ate their meal, they left the mud hut to go outside and set up for the preaching service. As they walked about, they noticed how the villagers were standing around, anxiously watching them. The villagers even began to back up as Arnold and Maurice approached them. Thinking the villagers were just curious about their equipment, Arnold and Maurice continued on with their plans and preached in the village that night. One woman, a village school teacher, came to Christ. They had plans to stay in that village for a couple of days, but by the end of the service, Arnold and Maurice felt there was such a spirit of hindrance there, they decided to leave that evening for their next meeting at a neighboring village.

They arrived at their destination of Zou in the middle of the night. The villagers were gracious and led them to their hut. Just as Arnold and Maurice were settling down for the rest of the night, they began hearing the beating of drums in the distant jungle. They knew this was the village's form of communication. A few moments later a teenage boy came running up to their hut. He excitedly told them that the chief of Zeregbo wanted them to return immediately. Arnold's first thought after hearing this was that angry witchdoctors had probably gone to the newly converted school teacher's house and ... His thoughts were interrupted and his attention was turned toward making plans for their immediate return to Zeregbo.

It was still dark as they returned. In the distance, they could see flames leaping toward the African night sky. When they approached the outskirts of the village, they realized the flames were coming from a huge bonfire. It looked as though the entire village was gathered around in a circle. As Arnold and Maurice walked closer, the witchdoctors appeared in front of them. They held up outstretched arms and told them to stop where they were because they were afraid that Arnold and Maurice's God would kill them. Arnold wondered just what was taking place here! Why were these witchdoctors afraid of God now?

He asked them what they were burning. They explained to him how they realized their gods were not powerful enough to even kill the Christians! They had put enough poison in Arnold and Maurice's meal the previous evening to kill six cows! Consequently, they were burning all their gods and fetishes. Arnold began to preach the Gospel to them right there and as Maurice interpreted the message to them in their own language, 27 villagers, including several witchdoctors, received Christ as their Saviour! They had witnessed God's love and protection of His servants with their own eyes and hearts!

Today, the believers in Zeregbo enjoy that same love and protection as they have established a strong and growing church, of over 300 believers, filled with faithful and joyful Christians!

The Lord has promised us that He will never leave us or forsake us. How true we have found this promise to be while serving Him!

**Episode 27**

# The Worn-Out Half Slip!

Our first Christmas program in the new church building at Abidjan was planned and prepared months in advance. We didn't realize the major work we would be encountering as we began making curtains for our first Christmas play. We stayed up for two long nights sewing those monstrous hunks of heavy, royal blue material. An American missionary lady offered to help us. Although it was Christmas, many years ago, I can still see it clearly.

Arnold and I both had to hold, lift, and guide the material as our friend sewed. Those two curtains ended up being about 25 feet high and 25 feet wide. After we finally managed to hang them on an enormous cable, we were set for the big night. Or so we thought!

I had practiced faithfully with the choir, and we were all anxiously waiting to share our talents. There must have been 500-600 people crammed inside the church building, and I can still feel the excitement of our first Christmas play. The choir was in place and I felt confident as I stood before the masses of black faces, dressed in my long pink dress.

The time came for the monster curtains to open – but they didn't! They were too heavy, so several people ended up pulling and tugging them open with their hands. What a riot after all that hard work!

The first verse went fairly well, and I was bursting with pride because of our accomplishment. That's when I felt it! The elastic in my half slip gave way and the slip started a slow descent to the cement floor! Our assistant choir director saw it first as it fell so gracefully around my feet. If I could have captured the shock on his face, I am positive it would have been used in a horror movie. I felt perspiration dripping on my face and neck. I had two choices: either I could stop leading the choir and pick up my slip while I made a mad dash out of the church, causing an even greater spectacle, or I could continue waving my arms like a good director and gracefully step out of it.

I chose the latter. By this time, we were beginning the third verse and I had my slip gathered up or should I say crammed under my left arm. The choir director had completely stopped singing and was staring at me. I felt I had to give some kind of an explanation so without missing a beat, I said, "Ooh-la-la, ma chose est tombee!" which means "Oh, my goodness, my thing fell!" The choir director never cracked a smile nor sang another note.

We didn't become celebrities that night, but for a long time after the play, missionaries and nationals always wanted me to tell the story of my worn-out half slip!

## Episode 28

# Attack of the Rabid Dog

Early one morning, I was awakened by Koffi, one of our African Christians, beating on our gate. He told me that his wife had gone to the maternity clinic to deliver their third child. Koffi had to report to his job, so he asked me to go to the clinic and said that he would meet me there later.

When I arrived at the clinic about 8:00 a.m., the filthy floor was literally covered with African women in hard labor. They wouldn't be given beds until the actual births of their children. Some were moaning, some were chanting, and some took their pain in silence. I saw how indifferent the midwives were to their pain. Had they themselves never experienced the sorrow, loneliness, and pain of childbirth? There were no words of kindness or comfort, only the command to hurry up and get the birth over with. As each baby was born, its tiny body was immediately submerged in cold water to wash it off. The baby was then taken to a table where it remained until its mother was able to climb off the delivery table, walk over and find her own baby. Most mothers took their babies and immediately went home in a taxi. African mothers were so used to this method that they never even asked to see their newborn babies. I often wondered if they got their babies mixed up in all this confusion!

A young mother walked in with her dead baby in her arms. The baby had been born in a taxi on the way to the maternity clinic. I asked the Lord to help me show His love to these African women who needed it so desperately. Searching for Eugenie, I was forced to step over several laboring women. Then I found her lying on the filthy floor with other soon-to-be mothers. I was shocked! She was almost ready to deliver. Then I heard a missionary call my name.

He told me to come with him quickly as our three-year-old son, Grady, had been attacked by a rabid dog. I told Eugenie that I had an emergency and had to leave. As I left the clinic, I kept saying over and over that I couldn't believe this was happening! The day had started out being such an exciting and joyful occasion, but now something had gone all wrong! When will I ever learn not to ask why but to accept His will as being the best for me?

The missionary took me to a clinic and Arnold was already there with Grady. The African doctors were working on him by giving him all kinds of injections. He had two deep bites on his face and another bite on his hip. The doctors couldn't stitch his face up because the bites needed to drain. We were told that if a rabid dog bites a victim on his face, he only has an hour or so to start treatment as the poison in the saliva goes directly to the brain.

It was only later at the house that I found out exactly what had happened. Grady Lee has always been the singer of the family. In fact, he could sing before he could talk. He was outside in our fenced-in yard with his back turned to the gate. The gate, which usually was kept closed, was left open for a few minutes by the African who was doing some yard work for us.

Grady Lee was singing, "What Would I Do Without Jesus?" when the dog came into our yard and attacked him from behind. The mangy dog dragged him out into the street, knocked him down, and started biting his face. When the African worker tried to kick the dog off, it only angered the dog more, and he got another hold on Grady's leg and took a bite on his hip. This time the worker got a stick lying nearby and began to beat off the dog and finally killed it. The dog's body was put into a large plastic bag and was taken to the veterinarian to be examined. We found out the dog was literally eaten up with rabies.

Grady endured the horrific ordeal of stomach injections every morning for 21 days. I saw that the Lord was truly with our son, as he hardly whimpered each morning when his daddy took him for the painful shots in his stomach. I'll always believe that it upset us more than it did Grady. He was excited every day because he would get a small bag of candy if he was a big boy! Even after that horrible experience, Grady loves dogs and has no fear of them.

On the same day Grady was attacked, Eugenie gave birth to Linda, a beautiful little girl! She was my very first spiritual grandchild!

**Episode 29**

# Linda Is Dead!

During the next fifteen months, little Linda, Eugenie's daughter, grew to be beautiful and strong. When we would walk into the church building, she would squeal for joy and reach for me. Needless to say, I loved her very much.

One afternoon, Koffi, her father, came to our house crying. I couldn't believe my ears when he told us that Linda was dead! She was only two years old. I had just seen her a couple of days before while visiting with her older brother in the hospital. It was strange how she had kept her eyes fixed on me that day. I had even remarked to Arnold that her staring and secretive sort of smile had made me feel uneasy.

Now Linda was dead! She had been sick for about twenty-four hours as her temperature climbed steadily. Cerebral malaria had quickly taken its toll. Koffi was on his way to take her to a doctor in a taxi. She took one last, deep breath and was gone from us!

Koffi and his wife, Eugenie, wrapped her lifeless body in a towel and took her home. Former tribal customs had taught them that a dead body should not be brought into the home of the living, so Koffi laid her tiny body in their small outside courtyard.

Koffi then came quickly to our house to share the heartbreaking news and to get Arnold. I was in a daze as the two of them left together. How would Koffi and Eugenie accept the death of their precious daughter? They had not been saved very long. We had been utterly amazed at their spiritual growth and zeal for the Lord. I kept praying that this tragedy would strengthen their faith and love for Jesus, and that they would continue in God's service and not give up in despair.

When Arnold arrived at Koffi's house, he knelt beside Linda to confirm if she was really dead or possibly in a coma. Her body was still warm, but as he put his hand under her nose, he knew then that she was not breathing. There was so much to do in the few remaining hours of daylight. Arnold asked an African carpenter across the street from us to make a small wooden box for her body. The sound of the hammer hitting against the nails was almost unbearable to me. Oh, how I loved her!

About 10:00 p.m., several of the male members of the church met at our house and accompanied Arnold to Koffi's house with the tiny wooden box. Linda's little body was placed in that makeshift casket. Grieving, they continued on to the cemetery. When they arrived, there was not an empty grave for her. The men hurriedly decided to bury her on top of another child's grave. When they dug down into the ground, they found out that if they placed the box directly on the other grave, it would stick up out of the ground. What could be done now? Linda had to be buried tonight as her body would soon begin to decompose. The only other alternative was to remove her body from the casket and lay it on the top of the other child's casket. As heartbreaking as this was, it was the only thing they could do. They covered Linda with a blanket and surrounded her with grass, straw, and rocks. She was then covered with dirt. This broke all of our hearts, but then I realized that Linda was not in that horrible grave! She was with Jesus! I prayed that Koffi and Eugenie would come to this realization also.

Eugenie didn't talk for several days. She refused to eat or even go to bed. She continually sat in the same chair, staring out into nothingness. Arnold and I sat by her side daily, reading the Scriptures aloud and praying for her.

Two weeks later, we held a prayer meeting in their home. As we were all singing, "What a Friend We Have in Jesus," I looked at Eugenie and saw the tears begin to flow down her face. I felt hot tears flowing down my cheeks as well. Although we were singing in French, when we got to the part that says, "all our sins and griefs to bear," Eugenie raised her hands toward Heaven in praise to Jesus. Koffi was also rejoicing and thanking God for victory in Jesus and His all-sufficient grace.

What a day to remember! These Africans, Eugenie and Koffi, who had followed their family's tradition of devil worship for years, were now saved, born-again children of God! They had passed through troubled waters and had come out on the winning side. Yes, there is certainly victory in Jesus!

Eugenie put her arms around me and began sobbing. She thanked us for coming to Africa to share the message of salvation with them. She told me that she could not have withstood the death of their precious daughter if it had not been for Jesus. Eugenie was comforted by the fact that she would see her baby again one day in Heaven. That same night, as I lay in bed, I prayed, "Oh, God, thank you for calling us to the Ivory Coast of West Africa. Thank you for your grace that is all-sufficient for every need!"

While furloughing in America, we received a letter from Koffi just a few months later. Eugenie had another baby girl. They named her Linda II. I could hardly wait to get back to Africa to hold her in my arms! Yes, even in death, we can learn valuable lessons as we follow Jesus and are led by His Holy Spirit day by day. As I write, Linda II is a beautiful woman with a family of her own. They are all serving the Lord together!

**Episode 30**

# It's Okay Now, I'm Going Home!

In October, 1977, we received very shocking and un-believable news from the United States. Our home pastor was dead! Arnold decided to send the three children and me back to the States for a month so I could be with our pastor's family. His wife and I are very close friends and we both felt I should go and be with her. At that time, Jason was 7, Valerie was 4, and John was 10 months old.

I had always flown back and forth to Africa with Arnold. My job had always been taking care of the children while Arnold directed the business part, such as passports, tickets, and getting from one part of the airport to another. I had the whole ballgame on this trip.

I was already tired and upset before we boarded the plane that would take us to Belgium. It was a relief to find out that our four seats were up front where there was plenty of room on the floor for the children to sleep. I then stretched out on the seats and tried to sleep myself.

About 30 minutes into the flight, the seatbelt light came on and the flight attendants hurried about giving passenger instructions. They told me to quickly put the children in their seats and buckle them in! That is where the scare began! Just as I secured the sleeping children in their seats, the plane began shaking and vibrating like a toy. I was so thankful that my children remained asleep and didn't see the horrified faces or hear the screams of the other passengers. I filled two nausea bags and began thinking how in the world Arnold would be able to handle losing all of his family if the plane crashed.

My attention fell on a handsome, young businessman who was sitting directly across from us. I had noticed him at the beginning of the flight, flirting with all the flight attendants. He would grab their hands and give them little pinches as they hurried about their work. Now the expression on this young man's face was one of horror and utter despair. He would grab his heart and then grab the armrests of his seat and squeeze them. It was obvious that he wasn't prepared for death. Just at that moment, a flight attendant yelled for another man to get back to his seat. He replied in a weak voice, "I'm too sick!" As the plane lunged, the man did a flip onto the floor right beside me. The flight attendant helped him back to his seat.

After about twelve minutes, the plane began to fly normally. The whole ordeal was over and my children never knew what had happened. I looked at the faces around that airplane. I had a strange feeling that many of these people would be thinking about death and eternity for weeks and months to come.

When we arrived in Belgium the next morning and left the plane, I looked around at the "big bird" glistening in the sunlight. Tears trickled down my face as I remembered the night before and the storm we had passed through. Our life is filled with many storms and hard places. Someone once said, "It's the calmest after a storm." Yes, the Lord calms the storm in my heart and fills me with His peace. I don't know why we have to ride out or endure the storms in life, but, oh, to feel the love and security of Jesus as He says, "Peace, be still; I am with you."

The remaining part of the flight was rather uneventful until we arrived in New York. Our 10-month-old had a bad case of diarrhea and had depleted his stock of old-fashioned cloth diapers. Just as the flight was arriving in New York, I removed my half slip and pinned it on John for a diaper. I was hoping I could buy some disposable ones in the airport.

I stopped at the nearest pay phone and made a collect call to my parents. I told them we had arrived in America safely and would be in Atlanta in about three hours. While I was talking with them, I looked around to check on the children, and someone stole my wallet beside the phone. It contained almost all the money I had, driver's license, and Social Security card!

I needed to go to the other end of the airport to catch our flight to Atlanta. I had less than 30 minutes and had just missed the last bus to get me to the Delta terminal. Someone told me I should get a taxi. I had a five-dollar bill stuck in my shoe, so with that bill and plenty of faith, I loaded the children and suitcases in a taxi. The taxi driver needed a course on tact and courtesy. As he was driving, he shouted out that the taxi fare would be $15. I told him I had only five because someone had stolen my wallet. He said if I didn't pay him, he would take us right back to the place where he found us. One glance at my watch told me that the flight was due to leave for Atlanta in about eight minutes. I began to cry. We arrived at the terminal and I jumped out and handed the man five dollars. He was yelling, and I was crying! A gentleman (or was he an angel?) dressed in a business suit stepped up and asked what the problem was. Through tears and trembling, I briefly explained my situation. The gentleman, or angel, told the children and me to go on to our flight. He would take care of the problem for us. Thank you, Jesus! Was this really happening? Three minutes to take off! I grabbed a bag and the baby. Jason grabbed a bag and Valerie's hand. We charged into the airport and up to the ticket counter. I was crying so hard that a lady working behind the counter ran out and asked what was wrong. I gave her our tickets and she picked up a phone, spoke a few words and asked, "Can you keep up with me?" I nodded yes. She took my bag and Valerie's hand. We took off running down the long airport aisles. (I was wishing I had been faithful to exercise and was more in shape!) We went around a corner, and at the end of the hallway I saw the pilot of our Atlanta flight and two flight attendants standing there. The pilot shouted, "Here she comes!" I peeked over my shoulder to see what celebrity the crew was waiting for and I realized that it was me! The kind pilot held out his arms and I just fell on him crying!

We went charging into the plane and all eyes were on – guess who? I fell in my seat and a lady reached over and asked in a heavenly Southern accent, "Are you all right, honey?" I smiled and replied, "It's okay now. I'm going home!"

After we arrived here in the States, I talked with Arnold on the phone and he was asking about our trip. He told me that the Lord had awakened him in the middle of the night as we were flying and he got down on his knees to pray for our safety during the trip! I wasn't surprised to hear that this was about the exact time as we were going through the storm.

I'm looking forward to another trip one day. I have the full assurance that my Heavenly Pilot will be waiting on me with open arms after I leave this world of care, stress, tears, sickness, and loneliness. But this will be a one-way trip and will be for eternity! What a day that will be! What-ever we must face in the days and months ahead, one day we will be with Jesus, and I know it will be worth it all!

Shortly after our return to Africa, we had another sur-prise! We had just gotten settled into a house in Abobo Gare and I found out that I was pregnant with our fourth child. I began to have excruciating back pains and severe hemorrhaging. I had a miscarriage and stayed in a clinic in Africa for two weeks. The doctor gave me several blood transfusions. I always joke about whose blood I could possibly have flowing in my veins. This was before AIDS was ever known about! This is just another example of God's mercy and protection over us in every way!

## Episode 31

# Hold On! We're Almost There!

As Arnold and I lay sleeping one morning in Africa, we were awakened by a loud banging at our gate and our dog barking wildly. Who was at our gate at 2:00 a.m.? When I finally managed to get to the door, there stood a French missionary who told me that his wife was in hard labor and she needed to get to the maternity clinic fast! They didn't have a car so they wanted us to take them.

I hurriedly dressed and ran out the door. Although this was the missionary lady's sixth delivery, the husband was very nervous and barely said three words as we bounced along the bumpy, dirt roads in our Jeep. When we finally arrived at their house, the husband jumped out and ran inside. I was nervous myself so I got out of the Jeep and walked around it a few times.

After about 10 or 15 minutes, the husband and wife came out of the house. I could immediately tell that we didn't have much time. From the expressions on their faces, it was difficult to decide which one was in the most pain. She was having one hard pain after another. I only hoped we'd make it to the clinic. Climbing up into the Jeep was difficult for a normal woman, much more so for a pregnant woman about to deliver.

Every time she put a leg up into the Jeep, she would have a pain and have to put her leg down again. Her husband and I were behind her pushing her up into the Jeep between pains. After we gave several shoves to the poor exhausted mother, she managed to slide into the back seat where she ended up lying flat on her back. Her husband and I were both drenched with perspiration, and I can honestly say that I have never been as nervous in my entire life. I jumped into the Jeep, turned on the windshield wipers, and took off into the darkness of the morning. The husband contributed his only sensible words during the whole ordeal when he said, "Linda, if you'll turn on the car lights we'll see better and you can turn off the wipers, as it's not even raining." What an intelligent man in the middle of such stress!

We were on our way, and the expectant mother's moanings were increasing with every bump in the road. I looked at the husband who never even looked back at his wife's sufferings. His blank gaze was fixed on the dirt road. At one time I asked the stiff body sitting in the passenger seat next to me, "What are we going to do?" His only reply was a cold echo of my own question to him, "What are we going to do?"

Well, so much for his suggestions. The lady's voice rose higher as she said, "The baby is coming!" I pushed down on the accelerator and managed to mumble a senseless phrase like, "Hold on, we're almost there!" Just as I picked up a little speed I heard a scream and thought that I must be dreaming. This had to be a nightmare! I was ever so ready to wake up! But it was really happening, not in Hollywood, but in Ivory Coast, West Africa in the back seat of our Jeep!

"Linda!" shouted the woman. "Stop the car! The baby is here!" I slammed on the brakes and tried to remember what they do on television when a baby is born before it is time. I got on my knees and peered over into the back seat and there they were! The poor gentleman beside me was still gazing into the morning darkness. I don't know if the next scene was normal or if the Lord just had mercy on me, but the baby began crying on its own. I picked him up and laid him on his mother's chest and covered the two of them with a piece of African cloth that the mother had brought along. I was so peaceful at this point that I couldn't decide whether to sing "Amazing Grace" or "Rock-a-Bye Baby."

We continued our journey to the clinic. When we arrived, the husband went in to get the midwife. She was a "big mama." She came out wearing surgical gloves and carrying scissors and alcohol. The midwife needed to cut the umbilical cord, so she threw one leg into the back seat, but never quite made her final destination. The new father and I once again used our strength and pushed her from behind up into the Jeep. What a sight!

After the procedure was completed there in the back seat of the Jeep, the midwife handed me the baby and I took him inside. They quickly examined both the baby and the mother, and within twenty minutes, all four of us were on our way back to the missionaries' house. I helped them to get settled before heading for home myself.

I could hardly believe my eyes when I walked in the door – it was 3:10 a.m., a little more than an hour had passed since I had left for the clinic. It seemed like an eternity. That was one sunrise I was glad to see pop through the darkness!

I was given the honor of naming the baby. I named him Aaron.

**Episode 32**

# Lord, Please Don't Let Her Die!

On a Saturday in July, we were visiting friends in Abidjan, Ivory Coast. While we were fellowshipping, our two-year-old daughter, Natalie, became curious about her surroundings. Without our knowledge, she climbed up on their kitchen table and proceeded to take a large overdose of malaria medicine. She evidently thought it was candy.

About thirty minutes later, as we were getting ready to leave, we noticed Natalie didn't seem to feel well. Just as we were wondering why, she vomited up a marble. We thought that would be the end of her feeling bad. We went home and I began to prepare dinner.

Suddenly, our nine-year-old daughter, Valerie, screamed that Natalie was shaking. By the time I ran out of the kitchen, Valerie had picked up Natalie and we met in the living room. Natalie's back was rigid! She was having strong convulsions and her eyes were rolled back in her head. I screamed for Arnold. He grabbed her up in his arms and immediately left in the car to get emergency medical treatment at Cocody Hospital.

Upon arrival at the hospital, they had the necessary medical equipment but didn't have any doctors available to use it. So off they went to the Treichville Hospital. Arnold had stuck his finger between Natalie's teeth to keep her from swallowing her tongue and by the time he arrived at the hospital with her, she had bitten all the way to his finger bone.

The Lord had already made provision for Arnold's arrival with Natalie. When he carried her into the emergency section, the doctor on duty was a small French woman. She had a daughter the same age as our Natalie, with auburn hair like Natalie's, and her eyes were also the same color of green as Natalie's. But that's not all! Her little girl's name was Natalie, too! Needless to say, these resemblances just knitted the heart of that doctor to our little girl. Throughout the night, she stood by Natalie's bed without leaving her.

When Arnold left for the hospital, I ran to the bedroom and began to pray. Have you ever tried to pray and felt that a big, black cloud was hanging over your head and that your prayers weren't getting anywhere? That is how I felt as I was praying for my baby daughter. I just kept saying, "Lord, don't let her die, please let her live." Floods of memories kept pouring into my mind. I remembered how I felt the day I found out that I was pregnant with our fifth child, Natalie. I had hung up the phone in complete disbelief after speaking to our family doctor. Grady Lee was only nine months old at that time and the thought of being pregnant again was more than I was able to handle. Then I remembered the love and joy that Arnold and I felt on September 3, 1980! That is the day Natalie was born. Her name means "joyful spirit," which is what she has been to us. We couldn't lose her now! I wasn't ready to give her up. As I began getting things out of the closet to take to Natalie at the hospital, I kept thinking that if she died, I just couldn't come back to that house.

By the time that I got to the hospital, Natalie was still having strong convulsions. When the doctor came out of the emergency room, I asked her about Natalie's chances. She just shook her head and said that it was very serious and that even if Natalie did live, she would probably have extensive brain damage and be severely anemic for the rest of her life.

In the Ivory Coast, medicines are not kept at the hospital, so the needed drug to stop the convulsions, Valium, would have to be purchased at a drugstore. One of the missionaries went looking for a drugstore that was open. More than an hour passed before he finally found some Valium. In the meantime, an African man came into the hospital with his small son who had drunk some kerosene and was also convulsing. The African man had some Valium with him to give to his son. The French doctor asked the man if we could use his Valium for Natalie, as she would die if her convulsions weren't stopped in the next few minutes. Graciously, the man gave the Valium to the doctor. They began to shoot that Valium into her little body, and by the time the convulsions had stopped, Natalie had convulsed for two hours and ten minutes. The convulsions would come and go in intervals of five to ten minutes.

Missionaries started pouring into the intensive care unit to show their love and concern. They all wanted to know what they could do to help. All I could tell them was to pray. I watched and prayed as Natalie's little foot would shake with the convulsions. She was lying completely naked on a metal table with no mattress or covering of any kind. On her right was a man dying with gangrene and on her left was a little boy dying from third degree burns. Two African orderlies were having a great time playing soccer with the huge roaches that were crawling across the floor.

The stench of that hospital is something I will never forget. It smelled of death and putrid sores. Each Friday, four, dark green, felt gowns were brought in and for one whole week, each visitor who came to see the dying would slip into one of those four gowns. We all knew that the filthy gowns were more of a health hazard than our own street clothes would be. I remember telling the nurse that mosquitoes were landing all over Natalie. The nurse pushed Natalie's bed about a foot to the left and began spraying insect repellent in the air for all the patients to breathe.

About three o'clock on Sunday morning, an alarm went off indicating that Natalie's heart had stopped beating. All the nurses and doctors gathered around her bed and worked with her. After about three minutes, her heart was beating on its own again, but she was put on a heart monitoring machine for the rest of the night.

I slipped away in a dark, damp broom closet, got down on my knees, and did the most difficult thing I had ever done in my life. For the first time I said, "Lord, I really want Natalie. I love her so much and I can't imagine life without her. But, Lord, if you can get more glory out of her death than out of her life, then I am willing to give her up." At that very moment of surrender, perfect peace and love flooded over my being. I felt God's nearness and presence in a sweeter way than I ever had before.

Sunday afternoon came and found us sitting, waiting, and praying. The doctor came and asked me if I would like to go in and hold Natalie. Although she was unconscious, I was told that she may be aware of my presence and respond. The doctor had put huge amounts of Valium into Natalie, so we all knew that she would be sleeping and unconscious for several days or longer. I put on one of those filthy gowns and a chair was put beside her bed for me. With all the tubes attached, Natalie looked more like a machine than a human being. I took her tiny, cold, naked body and held her close. I prayed that our Heavenly Father would not only let her live, but that her brain would not be adversely affected. I began to sing "Jesus Loves Me" to her because she always loved and responded to that song. My tears flowed unashamedly. I heard someone weeping over my shoulder and there was the kind French doctor who had shown so much concern and care for our baby. She put her arm around me and said, "I think our little Natalie is going to make it now!"

As I sat there holding my precious daughter, I looked about me and saw all the suffering that was going on in that long, narrow room where all the patients, regardless of their sickness, were lying side by side. I remember thinking how hundreds die in rooms such as these without ever hearing the Gospel of our Lord Jesus Christ.

On Monday afternoon, the doctor picked Natalie up in her arms, handed her naked body to us, and told us to take her to a pediatrician. We did this and spent the rest of the day where very qualified French doctors and nurses examined her thoroughly. They put us in a private observation room and we tried to give Natalie a baby bottle with water in it. She took a few sips and managed to whisper the word, "more!" After we left the pediatrician's office, we took Natalie home! She was still unconscious and sleeping soundly because of all the Valium.

For the next four days, we had to have volunteers sit by her bedside around the clock and make sure that she was still breathing. I will always be grateful to those precious missionaries who stopped their work to come and sit long and tiring hours with Natalie so that Arnold and I could get some rest.

On Thursday afternoon, Natalie started trying to wake up. She would open her eyes and close them again. She would try to get up, just to fall down again. We were all gathered around her bedside wondering what would happen next. After what seemed an eternity, she rose up on her elbows and saw her big brothers, Grady and John, beside her. She put one little arm around each of them, smiled, and hugged them close to her. We all started crying because we knew from her immediate recognition of her brothers that nothing was wrong with her brain. Nevertheless, to please the doctors, we had two brain scans taken. Natalie was perfectly normal. We had blood tests to see if she was anemic. There again, her blood was as pure and healthy as it had ever been.

You may ask me what I have learned through that experience. Well, I learned to appreciate my family more and to live one day at a time, walking with Jesus and trusting Him. Jesus makes no mistakes and as I look back over the past 35 years in Africa, I praise Him for each lesson He has taught us. I praise Him for His loving, strengthening, and guiding hand in every trial that He has brought us through.

## Episode 33

# Three Dead Ducks! "Ooh-la-la!"

I have always loved dachshunds. It was a very special day when we got "Fonzy" from a British lady in the Ivory Coast. This short-legged, black, male dog stole our hearts from day one with his unique personality. When he was in my lap, no one dared touch me. He made me feel protected and loved!

Fonzy was a real predator who showed us his abilities day after day as he hunted everything from snakes to rats to roaches. There was no fence that could hold him captive. When we would see him getting out of the yard and would yell at him to return, he would only glance back and run away faster and faster.

One day, Fonzy got behind the kitchen cabinet and ate some rat poison. I was horrified that he would die, so I grabbed the bottle of Pepto-Bismol and poured it down his throat as one of our sons held his mouth open. Arnold suggested that I pour oil down his throat, and as I emptied a quart bottle into his mouth, he swallowed every drop of it. An African visiting us said that we needed to crush charcoal into a powder, mix it with water, and force him to drink that, too. There was no forcing to it. Fonzy just stood there swallowing as fast as he could. Our little dog didn't die, but we could hear his stomach growling all during the next week!

The Frenchman who lived next door to us took great pride in the expensive ducks he raised. That is the reason I panicked when his night watchman came over and angrily reported that Fonzy had killed three of his boss's ducks.

Since the neighbor was at work all day, I had plenty of time to plan what I could say to calm his wrath. I was a nervous wreck! About six o'clock in the evening, I peeped between the hedges that divided our houses and there were the three dead ducks, all spread out in the garage so that the owner could see them before he entered the house. An hour or so later, his car drove by our house and pulled into his driveway. During this time, I was wishing that the ducks were still waddling around the yard and that Fonzy was the one spread out motionless!

Knowing what I had to do, I took a deep breath and walked over to our neighbor's yard. I clapped my hands three times, as is the custom, and I walked up to the house. The night watchman told me to go on in as he was expecting me. I could hardly breathe! He knew I was coming over to apologize! I walked up to the kitchen door and clapped my hands three times again. A male voice from the inside welcomed me and told me to come on inside. I was still a wreck, wondering if he already knew about the ducks. Maybe he wasn't angry after all.

I had entered the kitchen and was going into the dining room when I saw that the door was slightly open. Once again I clapped, and I was invited to come inside. The next few seconds will be embedded in my memory for as long as I live. The neighbor wasn't expecting me! He was expecting a female friend. He was standing there with open arms and when he saw me, his mouth flew wide open! He was completely undressed and unprepared for a visit from the American pastor's wife! I was so startled and so embarrassed that all I could get to come out of my mouth was, "Ooh-la-la!" Translated from French, it means, "oh, my goodness!" He must have shared my feelings for he repeated the exact same words, "Ooh-la-la!" Without any further words, I turned around and ran out of the house. When I got home, I asked a missionary friend to feel my heart racing because I expected to have a heart attack at any moment!

The neighbor had indeed been expecting his girlfriend and I guess the night watchman thought I must be the one!

We replaced his ducks, but I heard later that he told all the other neighbors that Madame Pasteur had come over unexpectedly and how embarrassed he was. That made two of us!

## Episode 34

# Delivered from the Curse

It has always been so easy to disbelieve and totally reject those things we have never experienced. I had always underestimated Satan's powers until we became missionaries in the Ivory Coast. This country is steeped in devil worship, man-made gods, and ancestor worship. In the early years, I would stare with disbelief as different Africans would share things I had never dreamed of, much less experienced. It was frightening, yet intriguing, to say the least.

We had a ladies' meeting in the home of one of our believers each week. An African lady named Cecile had recently accepted the Lord as her Saviour. She came to the meeting on Thursday afternoon and told us that her husband had visited a witchdoctor and had paid to have the curse of snakes put on her. I wasn't sure what to think of all the things she was saying, but I just stood there and listened. Cecile confided in us that she saw snakes everywhere she went. When she went to the market each day, she had snakes following her. In fact, on the way to the meeting, she had glanced over her shoulder and a snake was following her. Often when she was sleeping at night, her unfaithful husband would come home in the early morning hours, lean over close to her face, and begin hissing like a snake. Her dreams were always filled with the horror of snakes crawling around her and even chasing her. She slept fitfully and was afraid.

We were about 15 in number on that day as she shared these experiences with us and asked for our prayers. As I said, I was fairly new to all this, but I told the other women to lay hands on her and pray for her deliverance from Satan's attacks on her life. There was no emotion shown in that room after we prayed. There was no shaking or screaming. There were a few simple prayers and we all went home.

I had been home about 30 minutes when Suzanne, the president of the ladies' group, came to our gate and began calling my name. I could tell that she was excited and shaken over something. She told me that she had been the last one to leave the ladies' meeting that day. As she started out the door, Koffi, the man of the house, was coming in from work. They spoke briefly and she left. Suddenly she heard Koffi shouting frantically! Koffi was running out of the house so Suzanne went back to see what all the commotion was about. This is what had happened. As Koffi entered the house and passed by the bench where Cecile had been sitting as we prayed for her, a large black cobra had crawled out from behind the door. The snake slithered toward the front door and disappeared in the nearby bushes.

I certainly can't explain what happened that day, but I do know that Cecile was delivered from the fear and oppression of serpents. Her husband left her shortly after, and she was forced to return to her native village. She left with peace, joy, and praise in her soul, for Jesus had delivered her! Cecile was now perfectly free to serve the Lord with all her heart.

The Lord has shown and taught me so many things since June, 1970, when I took my first plane trip across the ocean. He has taught me that we should not and cannot put God in a little box. We must allow Him to work in our lives in any way and any place that He chooses. Hebrews 13:8 reminds us, "Jesus Christ the same yesterday, and today, and forever."

## Episode 35

# Can God Use a Cripple?

One special day, during the Christmas holidays, began like any other African day, hot and humid. I had stopped to take a break from cleaning house when I saw something crawling up the driveway beside our son, John. At first glance, I thought he was bringing in another stray animal to nurture and love back to good health. But after a good hard look, I realized this was no animal! This was an African boy! He was crawling on the ground, using his hands to pull himself along. At first I thought he might be about seven or eight years old, but no, he was 16 years old! His legs were withered and were no bigger around than a hammer's handle. His deformed feet seemed so out of place as they hung on to his small legs. Several minutes passed before he managed to pull himself to our back door. I looked down into the most pitiful face I had ever seen. His feet and legs were severely calloused and scarred from 16 years of being dragged along the ground. Because he had to pull himself along by his hands, sometimes he slipped flip-flop type sandals on his hands to protect them.

His name was Matthias and he had never walked in his life. I never found out if he was stricken by polio, another disease, or if he was born with deformed legs. I do know, however, that he had a very sharp mind and wanted to learn and be accepted like all children.

Since it was during the Christmas holidays, we had just put up our tree. The living room was decorated and the Christmas tree lights were shining and blinking. I watched as Matthias dragged himself into the living room right in front of the tree. As he looked at our tree, all decorated and lit, the biggest smile I ever saw spread over his face. He propped his face into his hands and remained lying on his stomach in that position for over an hour!

After that first meeting, Matthias was a frequent guest at our home. Every Sunday we went to his house and brought him to church with us. We lifted him up on the church bench and I watched him smile as he sang and clapped his hands. He always loved the services but I saw that he was embarrassed when we had to pick him up and carry him to the car.

Some months later, some dear Christian friends were overseeing the shipment of our Jeep to us from the States. At the last minute we had a brainstorm! Arnold called and asked that a wheelchair be put inside the Jeep for Matthias. We didn't tell Matthias our surprise.

The day the Jeep arrived in a 40 ft. container, we eagerly looked into the back and pulled out not one, but two wheelchairs! Neither was new but they were in good condition. Arnold jumped into the car and quickly went to get Matthias. I was so thankful I had my camera because I was able to catch the bewildered, then amused, then hilarious expression on Matthias's face as Arnold lifted his deformed body into the wheelchair. He didn't have to crawl anymore. He was somewhat awkward at first, running into one thing after another, but in a few days, Matthias became a real pro with his wheelchair. Things were finally looking up for this poor, crippled boy!

Later, Matthias made a profession of faith in the Lord! He then asked us if we thought God could use a crippled boy in His service! His heart's desire was to preach one day. In spite of being an "abnormal" crippled boy in a wheelchair, he kept on going for Jesus!

When our furlough time was due, we had to say good-bye to Matthias. We had grown to love him very much and knew we would miss him while we were gone. After we returned to the Ivory Coast, John went to Matthias' house to tell him we were back. He was told that Matthias had become very sick and was sent to his village. He never returned. Matthias died there. Later we found out the truth! His parents poisoned him because he was a "useless cripple!" One day we'll see Matthias again, and I know he'll be running, leaping, and praising God! What a day that will be!

This little crippled boy never became a famous preacher, but, oh, how wonderfully his life touched those around him, ours included. When I close my eyes, I can picture Matthias with shining bright eyes and always with a smiling face. I often think of him when I'm having a bad day and I'm feeling sorry for myself.

Can God use a cripple? I think we all know the answer to that.

## Episode 36

# Oh, Lord, I've Killed Him

Arnold and I were so thrilled when another missionary couple came to the Ivory Coast who would be ministering with our national pastors on the far-western side of the country. This new family, Jimmy and Jan Ammons and their twin daughters, lived with us in Abidjan for several weeks. We four adults got in our car and drove the eight to ten-hour drive to Duekoue to find a house for our friends to rent. We looked all day long and became very discouraged. One of the most difficult obstacles for a missionary is finding a house to rent and then making it livable.

We had almost given up on finding anything that day when we saw a nicely situated house on a hill. We all agreed at once that was the one! We couldn't see the owner of the house until the next day so we drove up to the city of Man and spent the night in a motel. The next morning, all the necessary arrangements were made for renting the house. All of us were exhausted after our busy day but we wanted to get back home to see our children.

As we were traveling along the main road, which is the only road leading up-country, all four of us were chatting and making future plans for the ministry. By this time, the sky was dark, and we were only about 20 miles from home.

I remember hearing Arnold say, as he was driving, "It won't be too much longer and we'll be home. I want to see our little chickens." He was, of course, speaking of our four children at home and our friends' twin girls.

The car passed under a pedestrian overpass and we immediately went around a slight curve. I saw a figure standing in the middle of the road. At first glance, it looked as though it was a man holding a light in his hands. I later discovered that, in reality, the man had an old, rusty, porcelain bowl in his hands. The reflection of the car light on that bowl had looked as though it was a light.

It was too late to stop! Arnold tried to swerve, but at that moment, we heard a horrifying knocking sound as the car slammed into the man, knocking him into the air. On impact, the man's foot was cut off, and his body hit the windshield with such terrible force that we thought his body was coming into the car with us. Once again he was thrown into the air, and he hit the top of the car with such power that it left a dent in the roof of the car. The next sound we heard was the body hitting the trunk of the car as it bounced off somewhere in the median of the road.

During this time, we were all very conscious of what had happened. No one was saying a word as we left the road at an incredible speed and began to slide on the grassy median. The grass was as slick as glass, and I thought we would never stop. I finally broke the silence by asking, "Arnold, can't you stop the car?" There was no response from anyone. During the accident, Arnold had knocked the car out of gear and that was why we were speeding and sliding in the median. It was the next day when we found out that the car had stopped only 15 feet or so away from an open concrete culvert! The

Lord protected us from going in that culvert at such a high speed!

The following scene will forever be burned into my memory. Arnold jumped out of the car and went running up the median, screaming, "Oh, Lord, I have killed the very one I have come to minister to!" An African in another vehicle stopped to help us. As he looked into the car, he saw blood on Jimmy's face and clothes. He found Arnold outside the car and told him to drive to the nearest hospital and get medical help for Jimmy. How Arnold drove those twenty or so miles is something I will never know.

We two ladies were in the back seat. Both of us felt something sticky on our faces, necks, and arms. We had small pieces of glass on us but no cuts on our bodies. We later realized that the sticky substance was pineapple that the man was eating out of the bowl at the time of the impact. I took my small traveling bag, opened it, and began to vomit as I shook uncontrollably.

When Arnold took his place behind the wheel, we helped Jimmy into the back seat with us. We tried to shield him from even more flying glass and from the wind. I never really got a good look at Jimmy during this time. I do remember he was holding his neck and throat. I pictured all sorts of horrible things in my mind as we covered him with a piece of cloth we had in the car. When we arrived at the hospital, our two husbands were admitted for emergency treatment. Jimmy had stitches on his face and both he and Arnold had small slivers of glass in their eyes that had to be removed. Later on, one of the doctors told us that when he removed Arnold's and Jimmy's contact lenses, there was glass sticking in the contacts. This is what protected them and kept them from possibly losing their eyesight.

Jan and I went in the hospital restroom. We took off our clothes to shake the glass and pineapple off of us. We bathed our arms and faces as best we could.

Arnold spent one night in the hospital for observation and Jimmy stayed for five days, as he has an artificial heart valve and is a free bleeder. When Jimmy is injured, he must be monitored closely because of the threat of infection.

The accident was reported to the police that night but they didn't go to search for the man's body until the next day. Investigation showed that the man we hit was mentally deranged and was never identified because no family ever came inquiring about his disappearance.

Arnold and I slept with the bedroom light on for many days after this experience. Although no charges were made against Arnold, he carried a tremendous load of guilt. A dear friend of ours had a similar experience years earlier. This missionary drove down to Abidjan to talk with Arnold about the accident. The two of them went into a private room and after a couple of hours, they came out with tear-stained faces. Other than the Lord, this friend was the only one who could truly comfort and help Arnold. That night we were able to turn off our bedroom light but we rarely mention that terrible experience.

The car was repaired and looked normal again. Several weeks later, Arnold and I were on our way to a church meeting when I pulled the seatbelt way out from the seat. Bits of glass and dried pineapple fell out of the top of the seatbelt. I began gagging and asked Arnold to stop on the side of the road. I didn't touch a bit of pineapple for several years. I can eat it again, but I am always re-minded of that frightening night of the accident.

**Episode 37**

# Look What God Has Done!

I was sitting on the last bench in the church when I saw her. The raggedly dressed African lady came walking in and went directly to the altar. All the way down to the front of the church, she was saying that she had heard God was in that place and she needed God's help for her baby. Was that a living baby she was holding in her arms close to her heart? I stood up to get a better look as she had entirely interrupted the church service. The small baby was motionless. The child wasn't crying or even whimpering and I never saw it move or blink an eye. She began to tell the story of what had happened.

The baby had been sick for several days. It hadn't eaten or drunk anything and had finally stopped moving. She had taken the child to a medical clinic and there they pronounced the child to be at the point of death. They told her the baby would be dead in a few hours and for her to go on home as there was absolutely nothing they could do now. They even gave the woman a death certificate to fill out for her child. That is when she left the clinic and made her way to the church in complete surrender to anyone or anything that could help her baby.

I watched her standing there in front of everyone, weeping as though her heart was broken. I remembered different occasions when I thought my own children wouldn't pull through an illness or an accident. She kept saying over and over that if God was really in that place, as others had told her, then maybe He could do something for her child.

Arnold had completely stopped the service, and several of the leaders, along with Arnold, gathered around this sorrowful woman and prayed for the power of God to come down and work a miracle for all those in the area to see. After the prayer, the lady left with her baby. I got a good look at her and the child as they were walking out of the church. Arnold told her to go home and give the child some food to eat and something to drink.

It all happened so quickly as she came and left that I didn't even think to find out where she lived. I regretted that afterwards but I kept praying that we would see her again. The service continued that day as usual, but my mind was on that woman and her lifeless baby. Early the next morning, we were awakened to a pounding on the gate. Arnold went outside and found the mother standing there with her child. She said that her baby had begun to nurse during the night and asked what she should do now. Arnold instructed her to keep nursing the child and to come back to church on Sunday to give thanks and glory to the Lord!

We didn't see the woman or hear a word from her until the next Sunday morning. A figure went past me and I saw that it was the same lady. This time things were different from the week before. This time the baby wasn't lying in her arms, lifeless. She lifted the baby up in the air with her outstretched arms as she trotted down the aisle praising the Lord and shouting, "Look what God has done! Look what God has done!" We weren't sure that it was the same baby as the week before because the child in her arms had put on some weight and was wiggling around and even smiling! Yes! Look at what God had done! The Christians all broke out in simultaneous praise to the Lord who touched this child and restored it to normal health in just a few days' time.

I always thought I believed in miracles, but now I know I do. I have seen the Lord do wonderful and miraculous things right there in the Ivory Coast, West Africa. I am glad, no, I am thrilled that I have a Saviour who not only saves, but He heals, consoles, comforts, and provides. Praise His wonderful name! I am so thankful to be a part of the family of God and grateful that God has allowed me to witness His miracles firsthand!

This child has grown up to be beautiful and normal. I knew God had great things in store for her life!

**Episode 38**

# Something's Chewing in the Corner!

I would like to be able to report that our first family visit to the village of Zou was an uplifting, spiritual blessing, but that just wasn't the case. We traveled nine hours on a narrow, paved road and then drove on a muddy, washboard road for over three more hours to complete the trip.

A wooden bridge had washed away so the children and I stood over on the side of the road for a long time as Arnold and some African men had to place huge boards across the gaping hole to cross. These boards came from trees that had been cut down by the Africans. They were about ten inches wide, about two inches thick and they weren't straight at all which meant that when they were placed, there were still holes between the boards! There were certain things in Africa that I just couldn't watch going on and this was one of them! I was shaking as Arnold had to place the wheels of the truck exactly on those boards to get across. After the truck got across, the kids and I had to cross the boards very carefully! My nerves were shot!

When we finally arrived in Zou, I was snatched from our British Land Rover by a mentally retarded young man called Domingo. Although I was somewhat frightened of him during our first encounter, I later learned to love him. Sometimes Domingo would wander around in our bush house in the middle of the night (as he did on several occasions). Arnold would tell him to go home and after giving a wide, toothless grin, he would leave, and we could go back to sleep!

Maurice and his dear wife, Angele, accompanied us to the doorless, mud house where we would sleep that night in Zou. I earnestly tried to hide my fear that our five children would be in a different room from us, separated by long curtains. The beds were made of bamboo and had an African material spread over the top. I quickly noticed that Arnold and I would be sleeping on Maurice's double bed, and we had two white sheets from America. I had given the sheets to him. I hated to grumble in my heart because this was Maurice's very best. He and his family moved out to sleep in another hut. There was virtually no other furniture in the house. Their kitchen consisted of a few dishes and a few large pots that were used to cook rice and sauces of wild meat from animals that Maurice killed when hunting in the jungle. Their food was prepared on top of three stones using charcoal and wood. This kitchen structure was separate from the house and had a palm-thatched roof held up by wooden poles. Of course, with no electricity and no running water, I had a time getting the kids bathed and settled in for the night.

Angele announced that my bath water was heated and motioned for me to follow her out toward the jungle. The bathroom was large pieces of bamboo enclosed on three sides and completely open on the jungle side. There was a large rock in the middle of the shower to stand on as you bathed. Each of us had one bucket of water so each drop was carefully considered. The Africans always took cold baths but always heated the water for us when we were there. Just as I got all soaped up and decided that roughing it in an African jungle wasn't so bad, Angele shouted that people were out walking in the jungle. I screamed a bloodcurdling scream, and Maurice grabbed his machete and came charging around to the bamboo thinking I had seen a snake. Can you believe Angele had played a joke on me? We all had a laugh and soon after, settled down for the night. I mean, Arnold settled down. He was asleep in about five minutes. Five hours later I was still awake. That's when I heard something chewing in the corner. I woke Arnold, and he said it was nothing and to go back to sleep. How can nothing make a loud chewing sound? I broke out in a cold sweat! My heart was pounding! I needed to go to the bathroom! I needed to go check on the children! I wanted to go home! I literally prayed that the sun would come up quickly.

I never did find out what had wandered in during the night, but as I examined all our backs the next morning, they looked like grilled meat with the prints of bamboo all over them. There's only one thing I can say about that first night in Zou - "absolutely unforgettable!"

## Episode 39

# The Sting of the Giant Centipede

I have often been accused of being a mother hen over my children and my husband as well. I was doing my duty on that sweltering day when Arnold left to go to the jungle for a few weeks. As he was leaving, the last thing I said to him was, "Don't forget to put on socks and shoes when you are working and cutting down the trees." He nodded his head and was on his way.

Two weeks later, the Jeep drove up in the yard, and I wasn't at all prepared for what I saw! Arnold's ankle and foot were swollen two or three times larger than normal. To make matters worse, the area was badly infected and oozing. I refrained from saying my famous words, "I told you so!"

Arnold's goal in going to the jungle had been to cut down trees and clear a place large enough to build his family a bush house so that we could all go out there together and I would have a private place to teach the children their correspondence courses. He had begun cutting down the trees early that morning. Naturally, he just had to be out there with his sandals on instead of his boots. As he cut one large tree down, the Africans began to scatter. It was only moments after when Arnold realized that the tree was covered with giant centipedes, but it

120

was too late. A foot-long centipede had wrapped itself around Arnold's foot and had already stung him six times. It initially felt like hornet stings, so he kept on working. By the time evening had come, it began to swell. The pain was so unbearable that Arnold could hardly walk. He stayed on in the jungle for the night, hoping it would get better. It didn't. He had to drive all the way back to Abidjan, which took more than fourteen hours, with his foot throbbing with every heartbeat!

I helped Arnold to the bed and I then called a Canadian doctor who asked me to bring him on to his house so he could check on his foot. When we arrived, the doctor lanced the foot and told us it would probably be better as the infection could drain out. We left with several prescriptions and went home. One of the prescribed medicines was a pain killer, so Arnold didn't even know when the phone rang the next night around nine o'clock. My sister was on the other end telling me that our dear mother had suffered a heart attack. The doctor told Leta to get me home if I wanted to see my mother alive. My heart has never been so torn between two needs. I hated to leave Arnold in severe pain, and yet I felt that I had to try to get to my mother to see her again. I have always leaned on Arnold and followed him as he made all of the major decisions. Now I was on my own. I decided to fly out the next day. Missionary friends came over and prayed with me. They volunteered to keep watch over Arnold so I felt somewhat better. After all, the doctor told me he would begin improving now.

I am sure I looked like a zombie as I boarded the plane the next day. Arnold was still in bed but he thought I had made the right decision. As the plane left Abidjan, I was crying like a baby. The first thing I did when I arrived inside the New York airport was to call home and see how my mother was. My sister answered the phone and told me she was somewhat better. What a relief! The next thing I did was buy three Reese's candy bars and ate all of them! I was so relieved that my mother was going to live!

I had just gotten to my mother's home and put my clothes away when the phone rang. The call came from Africa. The voice on the other end said that Arnold had gotten worse and had been put in the hospital. Gangrene was setting up in his foot! Surgery was a must! Arnold wanted me to stay on in the States with my family for a month and he assured me that he was being well cared for by the other missionaries.

During the surgery, they scraped Arnold's foot down through the tendons and all the way to the bone to get rid of all the infection. After a two-week stay, he was re-leased from the hospital! The Simrells, dear friends of ours, took him to their home and cared for him night and day. The children were settled in with different friends and seemed to be happy through it all.

Things went smoothly until Arnold and the children were home alone. The bulldog next door got into our yard and attacked our dog that was tied outside. When our oldest daughter, Valerie, began screaming, Arnold thought the bulldog had attacked one of the children. He jumped up, got his gun, and started out of the house. On the way, he lost his balance and fell down. Once again, he suffered from the injured foot!

It was a glorious day when I got back home and could once again take care of my family. Right before I boarded the plane for Africa, I called and asked Arnold if there was any news. He calmly told me Grady had fallen out of a tree and had broken his collarbone. I got off the phone and told my mother that everything was fine except

Grady had broken his collarbone for the second time. She wanted to know why I was so calm and didn't go all to pieces. I told her that when you have been through as much as we have, a broken bone seems like an awfully small thing to get upset over!

Many years have passed since the centipede stung Arnold, but even after all this time, his foot is still black and blue and he doesn't have good circulation in it. One thing changed, however. After that, he always wore enclosed shoes when he was out in the jungle. I told you so!

Oh, yes, I learned an important lesson in all of this, too. You see, no matter where we are or what we are doing, no matter what the conditions around us, God is still in control! He wants us to lean wholly on Him and trust Him with everything and everyone in our lives!

**Episode 40**

# My Personal Snake Selections #1
## (Every good Africa missionary has some!)

I had never seen a snake up close until we arrived in Africa. Once we got there, things began to change! I saw snakes in our garage, on the floor, and on our storage shelves. I saw black cobras crawling over the wall in our yard. I often sat and watched our dog, Fonzy, as he was face-to-face with a snake. Fonzy would stand so still and point until just the right moment to attack. He was inevitably faster than the snakes. Later on, we had two dogs, and what a sight it was when one dog had one end of a snake and the other dog had the other end, playing a scary game of tug-of-war.

We had just gotten settled in our African home and were getting used to the Great Dane dog we had brought over on the freighter with us. We found out that he was almost too much dog to handle. There was a huge field in front of our gate where goats and sheep grazed. One day, much to our horror, the Great Dane took a leap and somehow made it over the 7-foot fence. Thus began a wild chase after the goats.

I screamed for Arnold to go and get the dog. I watched as he ran across the field, but the dog had already disappeared. Suddenly, Arnold stopped. He immediately did an about-face and began to run so fast he could have easily won a gold medal at the Olympics!

Arnold had run upon a bed of newborn cobras and "Mama Cobra" wasn't happy. She reared up and began to spit at Arnold. That snake actually chased Arnold back to the wall in a school yard! I wish I could get him to move that fast! The Africans killed the seven foot long spitting cobra with a shovel. This experience was just another exciting day of our lives in Africa!

**Episode 41**

# My Personal Snake Selections #2

Storing our belongings on the mission field during our time of furlough has always been a problem. We were thrilled when a fellow missionary allowed us to store boxes of New Testaments in a wooden building on his mission's property. This was in a central location and easily accessible to the nationals.

After our year of furlough, Arnold began unloading the New Testaments. Several Africans offered to help him. They made a "chain" and passed the boxes along from one to another. Arnold was at the front of the line when he picked up a box just in time to see a large cobra rear up and spit at him. He jumped back from the snake as the poisonous venom zeroed into the national pastor's eye who was standing behind Arnold.

There was so much commotion by that time that the snake went back under the boxes and coiled itself around the wooden pallets that supported the New Testaments. Only the cobra's tail was sticking out. Arnold poked it on the tail but soon realized the snake had no intention of leaving its position. Another missionary grabbed a shovel. His plan was that Arnold would pull the cobra's tail and when it stuck its head out, the missionary would cut off its head.

Arnold pulled the tail, but nothing happened. Finally, he pulled so hard that the snake let go and both missionaries fell out the door with Arnold still holding the snake by the tail. Africans joined in and killed the cobra with the shovel and poles.

In the meantime, the African whom the snake had spat on ran into his sister's house. Arnold knew that milk was needed to neutralize the poison, but there was none to be found, or so they thought. The lady was a nursing mother, so she very kindly administered her own milk to her brother's eye. Thank the Lord the national pastor had no complications with his eyes.

Arnold has always been known to aggressively tackle a challenge head on. He does his best work under tremendous pressure. He would have died before he let that snake get away. I'm thankful because, if it weren't for Arnold, my book wouldn't have any exciting snake stories. I don't stick around in their presence!

**Episode 42**

# My Personal Snake Selections #3

Arnold and two national leaders had a meeting in Zou with the village chief and elders requesting land on which to build a church.

The meeting was held under a huge mango tree. Arnold and the nationals respected village protocol as they took off their shoes in the presence of the village chief. Just as the meeting began, a green mamba snake dropped off one of the mango tree branches and plopped into the middle of the group. Everyone gasped and scattered with the exception of Niki, a new Christian who had been strongly practicing witchcraft before his conversion. With his bare foot, Niki tried to stomp the mamba's head, but the snake was faster than he was. It lashed around, grabbed hold of Niki's leg, and sank its fangs into his foot. Niki reached down and pulled the snake off, and Maurice helped him kill it with a large stick.

Knowing the snake was one of Africa's most poisonous, the village elders began screaming wildly, "Go get the twins! They can take away the poison!"

"No!" shouted the chief, "Go and get the village witch-doctor. He has the power to heal!"

Everyone was astonished as Niki calmly stood there in the middle of the circle with his Bible held up toward Heaven. His words will forever be remembered, "If I die, I die unto Jesus, but if I live, I live unto Jesus!"

Several minutes passed, and there was no pain, no convulsions, just a peaceful look on Niki's face. The village leaders experienced the power and protection of the true God that day. When they witnessed that God had miraculously interceded, they were visibly shaken. The village chief was the first to speak after a long silence. "You don't have to ask us for any land. You can have all you want!" He had witnessed firsthand God's mighty hand of protection and certainly didn't want to anger the "Powerful One." A large piece of ground was given to the Christians that day. Zou has become the center of all the other village ministries on the western side of the Ivory Coast.

Many times I had quickly read Luke 10:10: "Behold, I give unto you power to tread on serpents and scorpions, and over all the power of the enemy; and nothing shall by any means hurt you." After the serpent's attack on Niki, this verse became alive!

**Episode 43**

# My Personal Snake Selections #4

We were visiting with our dear missionary friends who had just begun a work in the western part of the Ivory Coast. Their house was sitting in the middle of a huge field. We bedded all five of our children, along with their twin girls, on their living room floor. Everyone seemed comfortable and tired after a long and fun day together!

Earlier that evening, Arnold and Jim went to the back yard to check out all the commotion. The dogs led them to about a five-foot-long cobra. They blew its head off with a shotgun!

We packed up the truck and headed home after breakfast the next morning. Later on, the phone rang, and boy were we surprised, shocked, thankful and blessed after hearing what our friends said! After we left, a large black cobra crawled out from under their refrigerator! The kitchen and living room, where all the children were sleeping on the floor, was one big room. That means that the cobra was crawling around, or even slithering over the seven children while they were sleeping! We thanked God for His protection and watch care during that night!

## Episode 44

# My Personal Snake Selections #5

I have never considered myself a person who enjoyed camping out in the middle of the jungle. Being fearful of so many jungle creatures and critters, I always carefully looked around me before I went out by myself. When Arnold built our family house out in the middle of the jungle, we were all so excited to be able to go with him so that I could continue to teach the children their correspondence courses while we were there.

Our daily shower was a special blessing! The Africans would heat water in a huge iron pot and we would put it into our bucket, which had holes in the bottom, but had a cord you could pull to release the water to get soaped up and to rinse. The shower was covered with bamboo on three sides and had a piece of African cloth hanging over the entrance for a little privacy! Did I say privacy? That's a joke!

One night, Arnold was having his shower and just as he got all soaped up, a large cobra came crawling over one side of the bamboo! He only had one choice! Out he ran as fast as he could go still completely covered with soap! The Africans laughed about that for years after it happened!

**Episode 45**

# From "Terrorizing Witchdoctor" to "Transformed Witness!"

Arnold and I were receiving horrifying reports from the village of Bably. Our hearts were filled with great concern and fear for the new Christians there.

Our home church pastor from the United States, Arnold, Maurice, and some other believers had recently held a three-day crusade in Bably. Much to the dismay of the witchdoctor, 69 villagers had accepted the Lord as Saviour during this crusade. The Christians there immediately built a small, one-room, bamboo church building on the outskirts of the village. Other villagers began trusting Jesus. As they worshipped the Lord under the thatched-palm roof, the village chief and all of Satan's army could hear the jubilant singing, clapping of transformed hands, and praises to God! This caused a real stir in the hearts of those who had never heard of the Gospel, Jesus Christ, or the Bible.

Several witchdoctors and sorceresses mapped out their plans of severe persecution to put a stop to this new "religion" in Bably. They warned the Christians in person, by telling them that they must abandon their meetings. Of course that failed, so the physical persecution began.

One hot, sultry night, just as the services were ending, several witchdoctors entered the bamboo building with machetes and torches. The new Christians were so horrified that they ran out into the jungle where they slept all night. The small church building was burned down.

The next day, the Christians began building a larger and stronger building. Curious villagers were gathering with the Christians now and many were accepting the Lord as Saviour. As the weeks passed, those dreaded witchdoctors burned down the bamboo and mud church five more times.

You would think that the new Christians would have been discouraged to the point of giving up! Since the first meeting of the crusade, they had heard the verse in 1 John 4:4 that says, "... greater is He that is in you, than he that is in the world." They were practicing and living it as they patiently and joyfully rebuilt the church building each time it was destroyed!

The evil ones didn't stop at the burnings. They would hide out in the fields and attack the Christians as they started home at night after working all day. Several of the Christians' houses, along with their meager worldly possessions, were burned as well. Early one morning, Justin, the most feared and dreaded witchdoctor of all, went to the home of one of the church leaders. As this Christian man and his family were sleeping, Justin broke down the door with his machete and savagely slashed the husband and father, in front of his family. This man finally recovered from his wounds after a long convalescence. Justin was determined to put a halt to any religion other than that of his own demonic, evil-spirit worship.

One of the believers in the village decided that enough was enough. He reported the savage deeds to the state police. Justin and the other witchdoctors of the village were summoned to the magistrate and put in jail.

In Africa, the family of the imprisoned one is responsible for bringing meals to the jail. Our hearts were deeply touched when we heard that believers from Bably took turns every day preparing and transporting meals, over three hours, to the jail to show real love, "Christ-like love," to those who had so severely persecuted them. After Justin and his followers had been imprisoned for a month, the Christian wives even went to the magistrate and asked for their release. When word of these extraordinary acts of love reached the entire village, even more amazed Africans came to the services.

The next news we received from Bably was that Justin had been saved while in prison and his sorceress wife had also miraculously accepted Jesus. They were a shining testimony to all who saw the change in their lives. The village chief was so amazed at the changes in Justin that he called together the elders and invited the believers to a village meeting. Maurice took this opportunity to clearly present the plan of salvation to all the village leaders.

Justin told Maurice that he had to meet the white missionaries who had first brought the story of Jesus to that area. We were just as anxious to meet him, so we made immediate plans for the 10-hour trip to his village.

The main and only road past Duekoue was paved. After we turned off onto the bumpy, dusty, and hazardous road that leads to Bably and the surrounding villages, we still had more than four hours to travel. As we rounded the last curve in the road before arriving at our "bush house," we heard singing and clapping. Several hundred Christians from surrounding villages had come to welcome us. They had ingeniously constructed a huge archway of palm branches, large enough for our truck to drive under. Before Arnold could completely stop the truck, the door was opened and I found myself being literally pulled into the arms of one of the villagers. I later found out this was the converted witchdoctor, Justin. It was so hot as the crowd thronged all around us! I was soaking wet with perspiration, but no one seemed to mind, as they were soaking wet, too!

The next five days passed quickly. Each day we were invited to eat a meal in a different village. Maurice stayed by our side continually as we traveled from place to place. In one village, after we prayed over our meal, I opened the pot to serve my family and immediately realized by the smell of the sauce that the meat was rotten. I quietly called Maurice over to our table and explained our dilemma. He graciously cleared the table and brought some other food to us. The villagers have no means of refrigeration. When they hunt for their meat, it has to be cleaned, cooked, and eaten immediately.

I spent most of the church service watching Justin from a distance. He always sat on the front bench. I noticed that as he sang, he held his hands in a praying position, closed his eyes, and very often, tears flowed down his cheeks. This was 2 Corinthians 5:17 personified: "Therefore if any man be in Christ, he is a new creature: old things are passed away; behold, all things are become new."

Justin and his wife followed our family around faithfully for five days. Seeing his sweet, loving spirit made it almost seem impossible that only a few short months ago, he was persecuting the very ones he was now a part of and loved.

The villagers are always saddened when we have to leave them. On the morning of our departure, they all gathered around us to say good-bye. Justin pushed his way to my side. I could tell by his shining eyes that he was excited about something. His hands were behind his back, and he began a speech that we could tell was planned and practiced. He thanked us for coming to Africa and sharing the Gospel with his people. He then told us he didn't want us to leave, and with that, he began to cry. Justin said that he wanted to give us something special so we would remember him. Ending his speech, he brought his hands from behind him and presented me with a live but featherless rooster that was the scrawniest, smelliest creature I had ever seen! I was almost afraid to touch it. Then I realized he was giving all he had to give.

I am compelled to add a few lines right here. Observing the Africans for all these years has taught me an important lesson. Material wealth and possessions don't bring happiness, no matter how much or how little you have. I look around at these dear people, the majority of whom live in crowded shacks with many family members sleeping on the floor, back to back. They bathe with a bucket of water and lye soap. Most of them don't even have towels to dry themselves. They never know if they will be able to eat from one day to the next. The woman of the house usually prepares one large evening meal, almost always consisting of rice with a sauce over it. With so many people living in a household, it's not surprising that Africans may go to bed hungry almost every night. They have nothing to begin with, so when they "meet" Jesus, they find everything in Him! Fetishes are publicly destroyed and burned, lives are transformed, and then the persecution begins. Many times we have sung about giving it all to Jesus, that Jesus means all the world to us. Yet do we really mean it from the bottom and deepest parts of our hearts? We Americans sing about serving Jesus, but the Africans live out the words. God help us to wake up and realize the shortness of time!

After receiving Justin's sacrificial gift, I gave him one last hug, thanked him again, and we drove off. Scarcely out of sight, I asked Arnold if we could stop and put that smelly, bony rooster out somewhere in the jungle. I was gagging from the odor. Arnold looked at me as if I had gone crazy and said, "Of course not! We'll take this rooster back to Yamoussoukro and every time we see him, we'll pray for Justin!"

As soon as we arrived home, Arnold rushed to the marketplace. He came back with two plump hens to keep Justin's rooster company. That was the beginning of our new pets. We called the rooster Fred. I only had to go out in the yard, scream the name "Fre-ed" (in two syllables), and a little stick-legged rooster would come flying around the house to eat out of my hands.

Everyone who visited us complimented that "beautiful, multicolored" rooster who had control over our yard. (Justin wasn't the only one that was transformed!) Before we knew it, our yard had more than 30 chickens in it. Guess who was the ruler of the roost? We did pray for Justin many times a day. Each time we saw Fred and his harem, our minds would carry us back to the village where we had witnessed another "new birth" from a "terrorizing witchdoctor" to a "transformed witness"!

Today, Justin, his dear wife, and his children are faithfully serving God as elders in their beloved church at Bably. Many people of that village have accepted Christ and are spreading God's love in surrounding areas.

## Episode 46

# Daddy's Girl

The small, sturdy rocking chair continues to stand in the corner. Each time I look in its direction, I feel a very nostalgic pain shoot through my heart. Daddy and Mama bought the chair for me when I was only one-year-old. As a child, I sat and rocked and sang, "Bye, oh, baby bunting, Daddy's gone to work to get a little rabbit skin to wrap this baby up in."

When things were upsetting to me, my number one consolation and solace was to run and jump into my Daddy's bed and bury my head in his pillow. I was so comforted by the smell of Vitalis and Old Spice after-shave lotion.

Daddy and I often waltzed around the living room together to the sounds of Lawrence Welk and his orchestra. He was a very hard worker, selling insurance, so I saw him only at nights for a little while before I had to go to bed.

When I turned sixteen, Daddy and I went to look at new cars, for lack of something better to do. Mama could hardly believe her eyes when we drove up as the proud owners of a brand new 1964 Oldsmobile an hour or so later. I asked Daddy to take me to my band practice in the new car so I could show it off to my friends. Mama almost fainted and I received the shock of my life when he tossed me the keys and told me to take myself to band practice. He always trusted me and loved me unconditionally.

My teen years passed quickly, and in 1970, Arnold and I left the United States with my parents' first and, at the time, only grandchild. That was only the beginning of many good-byes to Daddy and Mama. What a heart-breaking airport scenario!

It is difficult for me to remember when Daddy was in good health. He loved to go fishing and I guess that is what bothered him most as the months and years passed. Severe emphysema and poor circulation took their toll on my dear daddy, and right before our eyes, this strong, hard-working man became a helpless invalid of skin and bones. Everyone who saw him knew it wouldn't be long until Jesus called Daddy home. His breathing seemed to grow more and more labored every day, and he often begged Jesus to take him on home to Heaven. Many times, he asked me what he had done to cause him to suffer so much. Daddy was on oxygen 24 hours a day for more than seven years.

Each time our furlough was over and it was time to re-turn to Africa, I always thought that I would never see him again on this earth. Our family had often fretted about the details of his death. What if he died while I was in Africa? What if he died while Mama was alone at home with him? Was the doctor correct that he would have a long, agoniz-ing struggle and that finally he would smother to death?

I have taught Africans for years about "Casting all your care on him; for He careth for you" (1 Peter 5:7). Why wasn't I trusting Jesus to work out every detail of my life and Daddy's life without worrying, fretting, and planning all our what-ifs?

While we were on furlough, my mother called me and said that Daddy was having some breathing problems even with the oxygen turned up to four liters. She also told me that Daddy had not eaten a bite in three days.

The next morning I drove to Covington and was pleased that Daddy felt somewhat better. I sat by his side and we chatted and joked about different things. I kept asking him if he could think of anything at all that he could eat. After several hours, he said he could eat a fresh pear. After we got the pear for him, he ate a tiny bite and pushed it aside.

My only sister and her husband dropped by that morning. For the past four years, Leta had devoted each Thursday to visiting our parents. We were all pleasantly surprised to see them drive up on that Tuesday morning. Daddy was alert and talking some but was having some discomfort in his chest. He kept begging my mother to turn up the oxygen. When she repeated the doctor's orders that too much oxygen would cause him to be comatose, he responded that being in a coma would be better than to continue suffering like this.

Daddy was saved many years ago, and I often saw him begin to shake and cry as he heard the old songs of Zion being sung on radio and television. He would join in and sing the songs he knew. It hurt so badly to hear him calling out to Jesus to come and take him on to glory and relieve him of all that suffering.

There was definitely something different in the happenings of that November day. Maybe it was the way Daddy kept looking at us, or maybe it was his continually begging us to turn up the strength of the oxygen. At any rate, Leta and I decided to go to the doctor and ask that Daddy be sent something to relieve the pain and be made as comfortable as possible even if it meant his sleeping all the time.

The doctor suggested that we call an ambulance and have him taken to the emergency room so his blood gases could be checked. We had all seen Daddy in a lot more distress and in a lot more pain. I never dreamed that in that very moment Jesus was working out every detail in spite of all our worrying and care.

As we left the office in the early part of that afternoon, the doctor again repeated that Daddy's death would most probably be long and agonizing. On the way home, my sister and I decided to pray that when Daddy's time came to go, the Lord would take him quickly with a heart attack, if it could be His will. Oh, how it hurts to sit and watch someone you love so very much trying to get his breath and gasping for air.

Daddy was more than ready to go to the hospital by the time we returned. The paramedics had no trouble at all picking up his 130-pound body and putting him on the stretcher. As they went out the door with him, Daddy told John, our middle son, that he would see him later on.

The last time I saw Daddy alive, he was sitting up in the emergency room hospital bed, and he asked me to rub his knees for him. About five minutes later, he told me to go and get Mama. As I left the room, a nurse told me that he was going to be put in the Intensive Care Unit and I began to cry.

On the way up to ICU in the elevator, Daddy began having one heart attack after another. When he arrived in the unit, they pumped his heart and gave him several electrical shocks, but Jesus had plans of His own. I will never forget the words of my mother as she took the doctor on duty by the arm and said, "Please don't hurt him anymore. If he wants to go on, just let him."

Mama, my sister, and I went on home, and what do you think I did first? I ran and jumped into Daddy's bed and buried my face in his pillow. Yes, the comforting smell of Vitalis and Old Spice were still there, but the body I loved so much had been promoted to a place so very beautiful and well-planned that my finite mind could never begin to imagine how wonderful Heaven must be!

There were two things that I had always dreaded in losing my parents or other close family members. One was seeing the body for the first time at the funeral home, and the second was seeing the grave and knowing that the body would soon be lowered into the ground. Walking away from Daddy's grave was one of the most difficult things I have ever faced. The blessing of it all was that God's grace, comfort, and peace brought us through!

When I picture Daddy now in my mind, I don't see him with tubes in his nose, trying to breathe. I picture him walking, running, and taking huge breaths from Heaven's pure, eternal air supply!

Heaven is getting closer and closer and more precious to me every day. I will see my dear daddy again, but most of all, I long to see Jesus!

As the choir sang, "What a Day That Will Be" at the funeral on Thanksgiving Day, I praised God in my heart for working out every detail according to His will and in His time. I wanted to shout from the housetop with the psalmist of Psalm 77:11, "I will remember the works of the Lord." Yes, those deeds are truly amazing! Thank you, Jesus!

**Episode 47**

# Our Coulibaly

When Coulibaly was seventeen-years-old, he lived in a remote village with his uncle. His parents and all of his other relatives had already passed away. He was out in the field one day planting crops. His uncle was bitten by a poisonous snake and just as Coulibaly ran to him and lifted his head, he died in Coulibaly's arms! Now he was completely alone with no family, no money, and no clothes. Coulibaly took his dead uncle's clothes and shoes off and put them on himself. There was only a little money in his uncle's possession. Coulibaly knew he couldn't make it on his own. He began to make plans to buy a bus ticket to Yamoussoukro (the city of lakes) and drown himself there. Coulibaly had no reason to live.

Arriving in Yamoussoukro, Coulibaly began walking around the town and pondering which lake would be best to drown himself. He was getting more and more despondent and sad as the moments passed. All of a sudden, he heard a voice booming as if it was on a loud speaker. He began walking toward the sound! Only the Lord knew what was in store for Coulibaly and Arnold that very day. It was the day the Lord called out Coulibaly's name to serve Him throughout all eternity.

As he followed the sound, he began to hear some of the words that Arnold was saying. Arnold had gone to the market place to preach that day. We had been praying about starting another church there in the city of Yamoussoukro. Arnold had taken his portable sound system and was standing on the top of our vehicle to be heard from a longer distance. He was right across the street from the largest Muslim mosque in the town. The voice that Coulibaly heard was declaring, "Some of you out there, within the sound of my voice, think that no one loves or cares for you and you are so alone and have no will to live. So, today let me tell you about Jesus and how very much He loves you and wants to save you. Will you come to my vehicle for prayer and counseling?" Who was this white man standing on top of his car as if he was talking directly to Coulibaly? Coulibaly came up to Arnold, got some information and accepted the Lord as His Saviour. He was transformed immediately! That was many years ago and Coulibaly and his precious wife are serving the Lord faithfully there in Yamoussoukro by taking care of our orphans and widows. He also helps the pastor there by preaching from time to time and conducting Bible studies. Yes, the Lord had a plan that day and we will forever thank the Lord for bringing this faithful servant of God into our lives! He has been Arnold's right hand man ever since the day of his conversion.

In another story in the book, I will tell you about Coulibaly having his appendix burst and he almost died. After the emergency surgery, he was told that he would never be able to have children. But the Lord blessed him and his wife with a precious baby boy seven years ago. "Little Arnold" walks around holding a picture of his white grandparents here in America. We have never met him in person but our hearts yearn to return to the Ivory Coast one day and be reunited with all our Christians! Until that time, we will continue sending money and raising support for our war orphans who need help so desperately. They need money for food, school, clothes, and medicine. Our hearts will always be in the Ivory Coast!

**Episode 48**

# Loving Your Neighbor As Yourself

If only you could meet our Coulibaly, see his flashing smile, see the love of Jesus and tenderness in his eyes, you'd know why everyone who meets him loves him instantly.

One day, Coulibaly came to our house complaining of excruciating pain in his abdomen. Arnold accompanied him to the hospital and after a brief examination, the doctors gave Coulibaly a strong treatment for parasites. Several hours later, Arnold and I returned to our house and found Coulibaly lying in the grass, writhing in pain. Arnold put him back in our truck and transported him to the hospital once again. After another consultation, the doctors decided his appendix had burst! By this time, Coulibaly was hanging between life and death.

After the emergency surgery, he was unconscious for two or three days. Each morning, Arnold went to the hospital to bathe him and take food to him. He would take a clean set of sheets and I would wash the soiled ones. As I wrote earlier, at the African hospitals, there are no medicines, no sheets, towels, or food provided. Each patient's family is responsible for taking care of their own and going to the pharmacy to buy the needed medication.

Arnold's arrival at the hospital caused quite a stir each day. Doctors, nurses, patients, and visitors would stop their activities to gather around to watch the white man tenderly bathing the young black man. I wish I had taken a picture of that scene. Bystanders couldn't understand how a missionary could love someone that much to care for him each day.

Five years later, a young girl had a pot of oil that caught on fire and just as Coulibaly tried to help her, the sizzling oil poured out on his foot. The pain must have been unbearable and the sight of the burned flesh covering his foot made one gasp!

Once again, Papa Skelton was there to administer antibiotics and change the bandage each day so that the burn wouldn't become infected. Now all that is left of these two incidents are the physical scars and an African heart overflowing with love for the missionary who cared enough to take care of him during his times of need.

**Episode 49**

# Rough Days Ahead

Arnold had just returned from a two week trip out in the village. I remember that he barely touched his dinner that evening. Although I always prepared his favorite foods for him after a trip to the village, I knew he was completely exhausted after sleeping on bamboo beds night after night. He showered and went to bed earlier than usual. About one in the morning, Arnold sat up in bed, grabbed his heart, and screamed out, "Oh, this indigestion is terrible!" I jumped out of bed to go and get him something for his heartburn. Nothing helped! After a couple of hours, I woke the children up and sent Grady, by foot, around the block to call the other missionary who was there working with us. Grady and Wayne came back to the house as quickly as possible. We made a decision to get him to the nearest clinic. It was still over an hour away! Wayne drove our truck with Grady and Natalie up front with him. We threw a mattress in the back of the truck and I was sitting beside Arnold. At one point in the trip, Wayne had to stop the truck so that Arnold could throw up! The pain was so intense that he was talking out of his head.

We arrived in the small town but couldn't find the clinic! When we finally found it in the dark of the night, all the lights were out and I jumped out to run in and get help. There was a stench in that building that I will never forget! I didn't see one person anywhere around. I was screaming that we needed help! No one came out. I ran back outside and then Grady decided to take matters into his own hands. He ran inside the building and came back out with a gurney. It was almost impossible getting Arnold out of the back of the truck and onto that rusty cart. By that time, a couple of irritated and grouchy nurses had been awakened, but there wasn't a doctor to be found. I remember looking out a filthy window and seeing Grady and Natalie crying as they slumped up against the truck. What was going to happen to their dad tonight?

A doctor finally came around but he said they had no medicine anywhere in the clinic. Even though Grady didn't have his driver's license, he had to drive around in a strange town in order to find the only pharmacist that stayed open all night long. I held my breath until I saw that Grady had gotten back to the clinic safe and sound. Thieves are out on the prowl throughout the nights in the Ivory Coast and I knew how dangerous it was for him to be out like that. The whole night was a nightmare and they put Arnold in a tiny filthy room with no sheets or bedding until the sun came up. We found a phone and called another missionary who came to get us immediately. We then decided to try and get help for Arnold in the capital, Abidjan. It took us about five hours to make the trip. I was praying the whole trip that Arnold would make it!

We were finally in a so-called "hospital" but the conditions were no better! The first thing they did to Arnold was to put him in the critical care unit. They wouldn't let me go in and see him. There was a small and filthy glass window where I could stand and peep at Arnold in the room. I remember the critical care unit smelled horrible and there were old boxes piled up in there beside him. They had him strapped to a bed. I was finally allowed to go in and all I can remember him saying was, "Linda, get me out of here!" What was I going to do next? The tears were pouring down my cheeks. I knew we had to get him on the plane back to America, some way, somehow!

The icing on the cake of this nightmare was when the doctors told me they were quickly moving all the ICU patients out to other rooms as there was a deadly virus there in the unit! A little while later, we were in another room and all of a sudden, bug spray started coming out of the vents. We felt like someone was trying to kill us! I was desperately trying to open the window just to get our breath! Sometimes you feel that you have reached your limit with certain things and this was certainly one experience when I felt that way.

We called the United States Embassy for advice and assistance. The African doctors told us that Arnold could be released to fly back to the United States. The airline then told us that Arnold couldn't get on the plane unless he was able to walk by himself. That was another hurdle because he was so very weak. For two hours before our flight time, he laid his head on a table and mustered up all the strength he could just to walk out to the plane. We were finally on board but would he be able to make the long trip from Africa to the United States? Only the Lord could have given him the strength for the long journey ahead!

Our family was waiting on us at the Atlanta airport. I felt like kissing the ground! We called the ambulance immediately. Arnold was put into ICU for over a week. It didn't take the American doctor long to see that Arnold had just had his first heart attack. They put in two stents and within two weeks we were on our way back to Africa.

The Lord knew that this was just the beginning of a long series of heart problems for Arnold! "Our Lord knows the way through the wilderness, all we have to do is follow!"

## Episode 50

# "Don't Look Nancy!"

Early one morning in the Ivory Coast, I glanced out of our bedroom window. I saw an African man running by with a knife in his hand. I screamed for Arnold who was in the bathroom and I ran to the kitchen. I remembered that I had left the back screen door unlocked. Just as I ran and latched the screen, there was a large crash and the thief had tried to get in the kitchen by throwing his body against the door. I am thankful I remembered to latch the door or the thief would have been shot by Arnold right in our kitchen!

I almost forgot to mention that we had five dogs that patrolled our yard. They were in a pen most of the day and we let them roam at night in our fenced-in yard. The gardener in our yard had seen the thief and he immediately let the dogs loose. I know it scared the thief to death to have five huge dogs running behind him! The dogs were very aggressive with strangers but were calm and loving to our family.

In the meantime, Arnold had come running into the kitchen with his gun in his hand and dressed only in his underwear! He ran out under the garage and by that time, the dogs had the thief lying out on the pavement. Our neighbors, who were missionaries as well, heard all the commotion and climbed up on the wall separating our two houses and were watching all the drama unfold. The lady of the house was peeping over the wall and her husband kept saying, "Don't look, Nancy!" Arnold and our son, Grady, were both running around in the yard with only their underwear on and never seemed to notice because of all the commotion!

By that time, Arnold had the thief hand-cuffed to a coconut palm tree! All around the base of the tree were huge, half-inch long, red, biting ants and were they ever hungry! We needed the police! Grady jumped in our truck and had to go to the police station and bring them back to our house. They informed us that all their vehicles were broken down. As they turned to take the thief in to be arrested, the police asked Arnold if they could use his handcuffs. We burst into laughter as they asked Grady if he would drive them all back to the police station. Never a dull moment living in Africa! So much for police protection!

**Episode 51**

# Saved, Just in Time!

Augustin seemed old to me the first time I met him. He tolerated Arnold, the first white man who came into the village of Zou, but that was as far as it went. He seemed pleasant enough when we would arrive in Zou each time, but his heart was unmoved by the Gospel and his mud house was filled with masks and graven images of his many gods. All of the villagers were shocked when Augustin's sons came to Jesus several years later.

Arnold and Maurice witnessed to Chief Augustin for more than 15 years. Arnold, Maurice, another missionary, and a visitor from the United States were in Zou when they heard that Augustin was very sick and near death's door. They went to see him and found one of our national pastors down on his knees talking to the old chief about Jesus. Arnold began witnessing to him again and before long, Augustin was sharing how he had tried everything to find peace and had worshipped man-made gods for years. He confessed how his life was drawing to an end and he wanted to ask Jesus to forgive his sins and save his soul. There wasn't a dry eye in that village house.

Two weeks later, Maurice came to our house and shared the news that Chief Augustin went to be with Jesus two days before.

That's why we "keep on keeping on" for Jesus. As we lived our lives in Africa, we experienced many joys and blessings, trials and heartaches. We have learned to trust in the Lord, and we know that one of these days when we finally see Jesus, "It will be worth it all!"

**Episode 52**

# Too Young To Die

Boto was born and raised in a jungle village called Zou (Zoo)! His father was the village chief. When our family would go to Zou for a couple of weeks at a time, my sons would go hunting with Boto. I will never forget the day when our sons came back from early morning hunting and had a huge dead monkey, holding it up by the tail. Boto's infectious smile and white teeth beamed as he announced, "Mama, this is our dinner!" I almost gagged. Sure enough, once the monkey was cleaned and cooked in a nice tomato sauce with new harvest rice, I forgot the first visual and actually enjoyed it!

I must add another thought right here on this page. In all these years, there is only one food that I have ever eaten that made me sick out in Africa. It was scaly anteater! We were out in this same village of Zou and I had to leave the table to go and throw up. The texture, the smell, the taste, the "everything" about it was too much for me to handle!

Boto was a born-again believer since his teenage years. He married a lady from the church in Zou and they had three children. When the war started in the Ivory Coast in September of 2002, rebels came to Boto's village and began tying old people to chairs and then setting their mud huts and thatched roofs on fire with them in it. The younger people, like Boto's family, began to run into the forest to try and escape the wrath of the rebels. Boto thought all his family was running with him but then he heard a scream. When he looked around, one of the rebels had caught Boto's seven-year-old son and was holding him with a huge machete up to his throat. Boto turned and screamed out to his son but he was just in time to see the rebel slit his son's throat! Boto and the remaining family members had to keep running and hide out in the jungles without food for almost two weeks, until it was safe to return to the scavenged village. This was the beginning of a civil unrest and war in the Ivory Coast after so many years of peace and tranquility!

Shortly after the death of Boto's son, he brought his remaining family members to our house for a few days. I can still remember the pain written all over his face as he recalled the terrifying and needless death of his young son. Arnold and I sat and wept with him, for his family, our Christian brothers and sisters, and for our country of Ivory Coast which would never be the same again.

A year later, we heard some more devastating news from Boto's wife. Boto had gone to the economic capital city of Abidjan to do some business and climbed up on an already crowded bus to get to his destination. A woman came running to get up on the bus. Boto reached out to grab her hand and as she climbed up, he fell out and was run over by the bus! I have thought a lot about Boto's life and his early death. Boto died as he lived! He was always helping others and doing what he could for the cause of his Lord and Saviour!

## Episode 53

# We Will Meet Again

I will never forget the first day I laid eyes on Biba (Beebah)! I was shocked at her appearance. She was probably one of the filthiest people I had ever seen in my life! It was difficult to breathe around her. I felt as if I was smothering because of the stench coming from her. She walked into our rented church building in Yamoussoukro and seemed to sink down in the last bench of the church. Biba had an equal look of fear and embarrassment about her. It was difficult to keep my mind on the sermon as I glanced around at her several times during the message. Later on that afternoon, I heard her life's story.

Biba had been married to a very prosperous and well-respected Muslim leader. He had several wives and lots of children. After he died unexpectedly, Biba and the rest of the wives had no one to take care of them. That is when she began visiting our church. She had followed the Muslim teachings because of her husband but now she was searching for the truth. She always sat in the back of the church, always wore the same clothes and always slipped away as soon as the message was finished. I was intrigued by this lady and wanted to know all I could about her. When her Muslim neighbors found out that she was visiting the white man's church

158

and listening to another religion, they threw her clothes out in the yard and told her to never come back again.

At first, Biba came alone to church but then she began bringing her baby. This little baby was born in very poor health. When I first visited Biba, I found out why they were both so fragile, thin, and sickly. As I stepped down into Biba's tiny room, my feet began to sink in the mud that served as her floor. I had been in some terrible areas but this one took the prize! Biba had absolutely nothing in that room except mud and a box of rags over in the corner. The smell was almost unbearable!

We began buying clothes, food, and soap for Biba and her child. I would go over and visit with her quite often and would always make an effort to make her feel really loved and welcomed at church. What a wonderful celebration we had on the Sunday that Biba accepted Jesus as her Lord and Saviour! Her life had completely changed and it was up to us to find her a better place to sleep and live.

Arnold and another missionary worked with African men to build Biba a large room made of concrete blocks, plus a spacious front porch where she could cook her meals. They also built a shower stall beside her room. Oh, it was nice and she was so happy there! Biba was always faithful at church. Her life had completely changed in every way.

Poor hygiene and living standards had taken its toll on both Biba and her child. Biba was a tall woman who was extremely thin. Her child was skin and bones from the first day we ever saw her. We weren't too surprised when Biba told us that her child was very sick and she was afraid she would die any time. We went to her house and prayed with her on Saturday. The child already had the death rattle! We knew it wouldn't be long.

On Sunday morning, Biba came to church with her child strapped on her back. The baby was barely breathing and flies were following her and swarming all over her because of the horrible smell of rotten flesh. Biba slipped in and sat at the back of the church.

The next scene will always be in my mind and heart! Our youngest daughter, Natalie, got up from her seat and went to sit right next to Biba. I had never been more proud of our little girl! Natalie took a piece of paper and fanned the flies away for the endurance of the church service. I knew Biba's baby didn't have long to live!

Sure enough, about three in the afternoon, one of our church leaders came and told us that Biba's baby had passed away. We went to her house to comfort her. Biba remained faithful to the Lord! She continued coming to all the church services.

Arnold has had three heart attacks. His first two heart attacks were in Africa. I will tell you more about it in another episode. While he was in the hospital, I went back to our home in Yamoussoukro (which is in the center of the country and also the administrative capital) to close up our house and get ready to take Arnold back to the United States for emergency help. When I walked outside our gate, there was Biba sitting on the curb and crying. She was so sad that we were leaving Africa. I put my arms around her and told her to remain faithful to Jesus and to serve Him as long as she lived. That was the last time I ever saw her. Coulibaly told me that she later went back to her home village and died there. I can close my eyes and see her as clearly as if it was yesterday. I know I will see her in Heaven one day! What a reunion we will have!

Biba's story is one of millions! So much suffering and so many needs in the lives of our people there in the

Ivory Coast. I wish I had nine lives to live. All nine would be spent in the Ivory Coast loving those Africans and sharing the Good News of Jesus Christ with the lost and dying! How blessed we have been!

## Episode 54

# From a Mother's Heart

It was 2:00 a.m. and I was feeling so utterly alone in a motel room in Zurich, Switzerland. I had tried to forget the events of the past 24 hours but each time I lay down to sleep, my body began trembling and the tears flowed like water from a broken dam. I had just said goodbye to three of our five children and left them in America. I was somewhere between the loved ones there and the loved ones in Africa, waiting on my return.

This was why I didn't want to be the one to accompany our son, John Wesley, back to the United States after his high school graduation in the Ivory Coast. The agonizing pain of the coming goodbyes surfaced many times during the one month I was there.

I had always loved Africa and loved the Africans with all my heart, but it came so naturally while we were raising our five children in the Ivory Coast. The time had come that we had been dreading for many years. Leaving our precious children one by one in America to begin their new and different lives, so far away from their parents, was the most heart-wrenching sacrifice the Lord had asked us to make.

Jason and Mary, his wife of two years, had come for several days from North Carolina, and our time together had been wonderful! The night before they began the long drive back to their home, Jason put his head on my shoulder and began crying. We all shed a few tears but tried to keep ourselves under control. The next morning as they drove off, Jason stopped at the end of the street to shout with a loud voice, "I love you, Mama!" He and Mary drove out of sight.

That began the most difficult 24 hours of my life. My mother was 80 years old, and her health was rapidly failing. I had been saying goodbye to her since 1970, and it got more difficult each time. When I was ready to go to the airport, I called my mama into the bedroom with my only sister, my daughter Valerie, and me. I held my mama in my arms and her tiny 110-pound body shook so hard that I feared she would have another massive heart attack. I couldn't help but tell her that I hated to hurt her so much but the Lord wasn't finished with us in Africa. She knows that, I know that, but it doesn't make the parting any easier. Mama turned her back and said, "Linda, go... just go on!" I blindly stumbled out of her house and started to the airport. There were still many goodbyes to say before I boarded the plane that evening.

Our son, John, had gotten permission from his employer to go to work at 7:00 p.m. instead of 3:00 p.m. He told me he didn't want to say goodbye at the house so he met me at the airport to wait for my plane. At the airport, he sat four seats down from me. All of a sudden, he jumped up, came over to me, gave me a quick kiss and hug, and started to walk away. I told him to wait and I would walk down the concourse with him, but he said no and with his hands over his face, turned and walked away. That was John's way of dealing with another goodbye.

The last sound I heard and the last sight I saw was Valerie weeping as her husband held her in his arms. I didn't look back as I walked to the plane.

More than 24 hours had passed and as I sat in the Zurich hotel room, I still couldn't stop crying and I couldn't stop reliving those final minutes together. I would be so glad when I was reunited with Arnold, Grady, and Natalie the next day in Africa.

I was so tired of people telling us that we needed to come on back to the States since there was so much work to be done here. I was tired of the same old questions, "How can you just 'dump' your kids over here and leave them? How can you give up your kids? I love mine too much to do that! Don't you see what you are doing to your family?" Then there were those who said, "You are doing a great job; everything will be okay for you as you go and do God's work." The thing about people telling us that, is that most of them were so involved in their families' lives that they couldn't bear the separation from their children if they moved to another church, moved across town, to another state or Heaven forbid, if they ever moved outside the United States.

By 3:30 a.m., I felt so much better after writing my thoughts on paper. I felt the Lord's presence in the motel room and I felt that peace that passes all understanding.

Yes, Arnold and I would keep on serving Jesus in the Ivory Coast of West Africa until He showed us another plan for our lives. I always told others that God's grace was sufficient. Now I was experiencing it, powerfully and fully! The Lord had promised us that He would never leave us alone. I was so thankful that He was with me right then. I knew I could get some much needed sleep!

## Episode 55

# Two Weeks of Horror

John, Nat, and Grady had just gotten in a taxi after eating lunch to go back to school. A man was coming up the road on a scooter at top speed. He had a woman in a long African dress sitting sidesaddle on the back and a tiny baby strapped to her back. Suddenly her dress got caught in the wheel and immediately she and the baby were thrown off the scooter onto the pavement. She was in terrible shape as the skin was scraped completely off one side of her body. She lay in the road crying. John told the taxi driver to stop, and the kids got out to see if they could help. Natalie took the baby in her arms, and John ran back to the house to get Arnold. They put the woman and the baby in the back of our truck and took her to the hospital. That was the last we heard of them. We never heard from her husband whether she and the baby were okay. I thought he might come back to say thank you, but he didn't.

A few days later, our son, John, was getting his scooter repaired at the mechanic shop and the mechanic took it for a trial run to see if it was repaired. He hit a man who was crossing the street and they had to take him to the hospital. By this time, we were all nervous about these two accidents. We didn't know anything yet! This was just the beginning of a terrible week to follow.

A missionary friend and I decided to take her little girl to a local swimming pool on Friday. Her little girl, Julianne, reminded me of Shirley Temple and I loved her with all my heart! I played with Julianne in the pool, nervous all the while because she had just learned to swim. I saw an African girl and a young man come into the pool area. He sat down in the gazebo before she got into the water. Since I was busy watching Julianne, I didn't really pay much attention to the girl except I noticed that she was quite stylish with a nice bathing suit. I was near the ladder with Julianne when I felt something brush up against me. I looked down and saw the African girl swimming underwater on her side, moving her arms and legs in a swimming motion. She tapped me again, and I looked at Nancy and said, "What is she doing?" Nancy and I both thought she was just showing off in front of the man who came with her. I realized later that she was having a seizure.

About that time, little Julianne decided she wanted to go over to the baby pool, so I watched her climb out. Nancy and I swam out to the deep end and talked for a while. When we swam back to the other side, the African girl was floating on her stomach under the water. We looked up at the man who had come with her, and he was still sitting there grinning and watching her. Nancy asked him if she could swim, and he replied that she was a good swimmer. I asked him why she wasn't moving, and he got up from the chair and said for us to lift her up. I still thought she was playing, so I told Nancy to lift her up. We both expected her to look up and ask what we were doing. As soon as Nancy touched her, we knew she had drowned. The man with her ran off and didn't come back for at least 30 minutes until needed help arrived. Nancy pulled her to the ladder and I got out of the water and tried to pull the body out. Nancy pushed her from behind, and I pulled on her arms, but she was quite heavy, and her legs kept falling back in the water.

There was supposedly a lifeguard there who had gone to get change, and when he came back and saw what was going on, all he could do was walk in circles and scream, "My God!" Four other women were sitting by the pool just staring at everything, but not one of them offered to help Nancy and me. I was screaming all this time and begging someone to come help us.

We finally got the girl out of the pool and put her on her back but immediately saw that she wasn't breathing. Nancy began to pump her heart, and in a minute or so, the girl started breathing again but it wasn't normal. Twenty minutes later, the ambulance came up and the paramedics (at least that's what they called themselves) walked as slowly to the pool as if they were on a sight-seeing tour. They really didn't do anything for her. At one time she tried to raise herself up off the mat and made a moaning sound. Paramedics watched her for a few minutes, then wrapped her in a blanket and took her to the Yamoussoukro hospital.

Nancy and I sat there a long time shaking and talking about what we should have done. You never know how you'll react in a situation like that until it happens to you. I called the lifeguard over and asked why he didn't help us. I also asked him if he knew how to give CPR. He looked me straight in the eyes and said he knew how to do all of that but that he was gone to get change when we were pulling the girl out of the pool. That was not true. Nancy and I both saw him standing there looking but he didn't do anything to help.

That night Nancy came over to the house. We were still very shaken up. Arnold was gone to a meeting of the national pastors in Abidjan, and Nancy's husband was out of town, too. I slept with the light on because I kept seeing that girl's face every time I closed my eyes. I told

Nancy what a shame it would be to have saved the girl from physical death and then her die and go to hell one day. I promised the Lord that I would go to the hospital early the next morning to find the girl and tell her about Jesus. At seven the next morning, I walked to the hospital and found out that she had been transferred to Bouake the night before. I asked if she was okay, and they said they thought she was but they didn't have the needed equipment to take care of her. I asked for her address in Yamoussoukro, and they didn't know it, but they did give me the name of the school where her aunt taught. I got in a taxi and the driver told me the school was about 7 miles outside of Yamoussoukro. I told him why I had to find her house and said I was willing to pay him well if he would help me. We went to the school first and found out where the young lady lived. A man came walking out to the gate and he was crying. He had just gotten word that the girl had died at the Bouake hospital. I began crying and told him why I had come to find her that morning. He said he would call me and let me know when the funeral was but I didn't hear from him again.

After hearing this upsetting news, I asked the taxi driver to make one more stop for me at the market before going home. I bought three ignames and told him I wanted to give them to someone. (An igname is an extremely starchy African vegetable, similar to a potato.) There was a little white-haired African lady who lived up on the corner of our road. Everyone thought she was crazy but she was just senile. I had talked to her many times and she was very polite and spoke very good French. She had cleaned up that whole corner and always prepared food on three little stones. She raked up straw into neat little piles and set fire to it every night. All her earthly possessions were around her. She always wore clothes, but they were rags.

As we were going toward our house, I saw the little woman walking up the road. I said, "Stop, there she is." The taxi driver told me she was crazy. I assured him that I wanted to stop anyway. He made a U-turn and I got out to give her the ignames. She did a little bow and thanked me and thanked me. I asked her if she wanted me to take them to the corner, and she whispered to me that there were thieves there and to just put them in the bushes and she would get them later. I got back into the taxi. All this time, the taxi driver kept looking at me as if to say, "What kind of crazy white woman are you?" We drove up to the house, and I gave him 2,000 francs. He told me that he was only going to charge me 1,000. I thanked him and as I turned to go into the yard, he called me and said, "Madame, I have to tell you, this is the strangest day of my life." I just laughed and told him I felt the same way.

Later that week, Arnold and I had been to Abidjan so I could see the dentist, and on the way back up the main road in the country, we saw a big bus that had just wrecked and was on its side. Some people were still inside the bus. We stopped and asked a policeman if we could do anything. He answered that if we could go ahead and transport the most injured ones to the hospital, then that would be a big help. I must tell you, I was scared to even look at them.

We found out that the front tire on the bus had blown out and the driver lost control. Thank the Lord no one was killed, but there were a lot of injured people on the side of the road. Arnold immediately took out his medical box and began bandaging as many as he could. They put one man in the back of our truck whose hand was completely cut off. His friend told me that the bus had flipped over on its side and had almost completely cut the hand off except for a few pieces of skin. The friend had taken a piece of broken window and cut the loose skin off to free the man. His hand was still trapped under the bus. He was in terrible pain, but he never screamed out loud!

There was another man with a cut from the top of his head to his ear and that was a terrible sight. He got in the truck also. There was another man covered in blood that had cut his legs badly and he could hardly walk. In all, there were four in our truck who were critically wounded. The policeman climbed up in front with Arnold and me, and we went about 30 kilometers back toward Abidjan to the nearest hospital. Did I say hospital? It was a nightmare to say the least. When we arrived at the hospital, the injured people were taken inside and placed on the floor – and nasty it was! The man with the hand cut off was going into shock and yet he kept thanking Arnold for saving his life, and was even asking where we lived so he could come to our house and thank us after he got better. Arnold was standing there in the middle of all those suffering people with his arms up in the air and began praying in a loud voice for them. There were two lady nurses there who were Christians and they thanked us for helping the accident victims and for praying for them, too. When we left the hospital, the doctors had not begun working on the poor wounded people.

We went back to the scene of the accident and Arnold got out to see if there was anything else he could do. He walked over to the wrecked bus and was looking for something. I knew immediately that he was looking for that man's hand. It was hidden and still trapped under the bus, but if Arnold had found it, he would have taken it to the hospital to see if that man's hand could be saved. We were both upset about all that and went to bed early that night. The next morning Arnold took the truck and had it completely disinfected and scrubbed. Blood was everywhere in the back!

Last but not least, I had gone to bed early one night. Usually I got up at six in the morning and by nine at night I was always zapped. Arnold woke me up, calling my name, and said he thought John had been bitten by a snake. I was always telling the children to put on their shoes when they went outside. John had gone up to lock the gate in the dark and he had two holes on the end of his toe which were definitely either a snake or a spider bite. It scared us to death, but Arnold had his snake bite suction kit that was amazing. He put that on the end of John's toe and it sucked that toe way out. You could see what looked like water and blood coming out of those two fang bites. We kept a close eye on John all night. Arnold and I kept going in there to check on him and wake him up to ask if he felt any pain. He felt okay and slept well.

Well, this is just a glimpse into the two weeks of horror. I was praying and hoping that things would go smoother for a while. There in Africa you never know what tomorrow may bring!

**Episode 56**

# Hit the Floor!

Our middle son, John Wesley, had come to the Ivory Coast to visit us in September of 2003. John was in the U.S. Navy and had a couple of weeks of leave time. The first week for John was filled with seeing old friends and visiting familiar places there in his country of birth.

Arnold, John, and I were standing out on our screened porch when we heard bullets whizzing by our house and trees. Some were even hitting the walls around our house. Arnold screamed out, "Hit the floor!" I literally crawled back to our bedroom. I know that must have been the most surprising and frightening moments of my life!

We had only known peace and freedom in the Ivory Coast. Each part of our ministry had begun by going into a new area, having the liberty to preach in the open air and thus begin a church with the new converts that had heard the Gospel. I have never liked any kind of change. Most people don't, and the Ivory Coast, as we had always known it, changed drastically that day. As we were in our beds on that first night, we could hear helicopters and planes going over the house. There wasn't much sleep for us but we were in prayer asking the Lord for protection for other missionaries, our African family, and ourselves.

Civil war within a country seems to be the worst kind. The Bible teaches in Mark 3:25, "And if a house be divided against itself, that house cannot stand." Neither can a country! We were praying that the country would settle down in a few days and that all would be back to normal. As I sat writing this story, almost five years had passed and the country was still torn apart. The Ivory Coast was literally divided in half. As the country was torn in two, so were our hearts. We just praise the Lord for 35 years of freedom in open-air preaching and teaching there in our beloved Ivory Coast!

Ivory Coast now has a democratic form of government and we are so thankful that the Civil War has ended. Prosperity is returning to the Ivory Coast!

**Episode 57**

# Uncertain Days

Yes, civil war had officially begun in our beloved Ivory Coast! We were afraid the airport would close and that our son, John, wouldn't be able to leave the Ivory Coast to go back to America where he was currently serving in the United States Navy. He had a specific time to be back from leave. We immediately began making plans to get him back to the capital of the Ivory Coast, which takes about three hours from where we live in the center of the country. Arnold told me that it wasn't safe to travel and I should stay home while he escorted John. Then, all of a sudden, Arnold changed his mind and told me to pack a bag for myself.

The three of us began the trip to Abidjan. Before leaving our town of Yamoussoukro, we were stopped in a line of traffic and noticed that the police were searching all vehicles and making people get out of their car to be frisked. We weren't worried! We didn't have anything to hide, or did we? Yep, there it was under Arnold's seat, our tiny pistol! Just as we remembered that we even had it in the car, it was our turn to drive up to the police officers. Arnold was frantically trying to pass the pistol to John and then back to me to hide it in the back seat. As I touched the pistol, I was shaking uncontrollably as I slipped it under my floor mat in the back seat. The police officers made Arnold get out of the car and he was frisked from head to foot. They didn't check the inside of the car.

If you could have seen the three of us passing that little pistol like a hot potato, you would have burst into laughter! We laugh now but it wasn't at all amusing at the time! John was able to get out on the flight back to America and my heart broke as we said yet another good-bye, especially in the face of such uncertainty.

Later on in the morning, we found out that gasoline and diesel fuel were almost impossible to find. Arnold and I had slept at a missionary guesthouse for a couple of days when he dropped the bombshell on me! I remember Arnold began crying and saying that he must drive back home to Yamoussoukro because he couldn't leave the Africans without any food or money. All of the other missionaries were pleading with Arnold to stay in Abidjan because traveling upcountry was very dangerous. I was so upset and I also begged him to stay with me to at least be near the airport in case of an evacuation. In case I didn't tell you readers before, when Arnold says the Lord has spoken to him, there is no stopping him. I should have realized after all those years of living with him that he was going to obey the Lord, no matter what the cost!

The next day Arnold found a gas station that still had some fuel so he filled up our gas tank and also filled up three plastic gas containers to get him to Yamoussoukro and back. Even before getting out of Abidjan, Arnold had to pass three police barricades. The policemen and soldiers were stopping every car and checking for hidden fuel! We had extra fuel but it certainly wasn't hidden! The first miracle took place as Arnold was stopped and told to open the back of the truck. There were three bright red fuel containers sitting there and yet the soldier's eyes were literally blinded from seeing them! This same thing happened at three different stops!

As he continued on his journey, he decided to stop on the side of the road and fill up the truck's tank with the extra diesel fuel in the back. He poured the fuel in and got back in the truck. About fifty miles up the road, he happened to glance in his rearview mirror and saw that the fuel tank cover was wide open and the lid was gone! Panic and disbelief rose up inside him! Arnold immediately stopped and was trying to figure out what cloth he could stuff in the tank to preserve the diesel fuel and you won't believe what happened, or will you? Miracle number two transpired! There on the very edge of the top of the truck was the small and very light fuel lid cover! Even as I sit writing, I can just picture those "angels" sitting inside and on top of that truck protecting Arnold every step of the way!

Shortly up the road, Arnold was able to stop in a village and fill the truck with charcoal, sacks of rice, and plantain bananas. He spent twenty-four hours at our house in Yamoussoukro and all night long, he distributed food, money, and got our house all locked up. When he returned to Abidjan the next day, he didn't say two words. He was exhausted mentally and physically! He went to sleep and woke me early the next morning to say that he felt that we should try and get a flight out to America that very day!

## Episode 58

# Traveling Nightmares

Traveling to the airport was a nightmare! There were literally hundreds of scared and rioting Africans marching up the middle of the main road. We just happened to be at the end of the marching crowd so we went very slowly until we could get around them. We later heard stories about angry mobs literally pulling people out of their cars and harassing them in different ways. Tension was running high and we saw two fist fights erupt while we were waiting outside the airport doors. Everyone was nervously and impatiently waiting to get a flight out of the country.

The Lord blessed us and we were able to use our stand-by tickets to get on the first flight of the evening. While standing in line to board the plane, we made a couple of teary phone calls to say goodbye to our African Christians back in Yamoussoukro. I will never forget the last sentence I heard before boarding the plane. A soldier looked at us and said, "Oh, we hate to see you missionaries leaving us!" Arnold and I both wept like babies as the plane climbed and we looked down at the country where we had served and loved for so many years.

There were horrific stories told on our airplane of how some French nationals had to stay in their homes for several weeks and had to drink the water in their swimming pools. One French man sitting next to me on the plane told how he found himself in the middle of an angry mob as he was driving to the airport to try and get a flight. He had been dragged from his car but managed to escape. This Frenchman was still crying and shaking on the plane several hours after his ordeal.

## Episode 59

# That Man Stole My Briefcase!

After arriving in France, our tribulations were continuing. We waited all day long and couldn't get a flight out of Paris to America. Hungry, physically and mentally exhausted, we got a shuttle and went to a cheap hotel. In the lobby, there were many people standing around. As Arnold checked on a room for us, I stood to the side and carefully guarded our luggage. We had already been warned that thieves were rampant in that part of town.

All at once, a Frenchman standing at the check-in desk began screaming at Arnold and accusing him of stealing his briefcase which had been on the floor next to him seconds earlier. We had been through so much both physically and emotionally during the last two weeks and now this accusation and in front of everyone! My mouth fell open during the whole scenario. Arnold just stood there looking at him in disbelief!

Thank the Lord for inside cameras because the hotel manager rushed to his office and replayed the hidden tapes. On the tape, we saw a woman come in the hotel lobby and stand there between the French man and Arnold. Moments later, a small boy about six years old walked in, picked up the briefcase and exited the lobby. The woman followed shortly afterwards. Case closed? Not quite! We were warned to go to our room and stay there with our luggage as there had been several robberies there in that hotel in recent days. That same night, two American women had their money and passports stolen from their rooms.

By the time we arrived in America, we had literally been traveling for three days. Arnold and I felt like we were zombies. What a trip! I later realized that during the trip home, the song, "The Lord knows the way through the wilderness" kept flooding my thoughts. "Lord, help us to never forget that you do know the way through every trial and every situation and all we have to do is follow. Thank you for leading your children!"

Our five children were concerned about us when we got home. We just sat around and didn't talk much at all for the first few days back in Georgia. After several days of rest and reflection, we were feeling more like our old selves. We were back in our home state, but a huge portion of our hearts remained in the Ivory Coast. Now several years have passed and we can honestly say that our love and burden for the Ivory Coast just grows stronger with each passing day.

**Episode 60**

# Heart Attack Number 2

For those who don't know, we have been back in the States since 2004. That is the year when Arnold had his second heart attack. It seems that his health has been deteriorating ever since.

Since we left the field, our hearts have been so burdened about helping the poor war orphans and widows there in the Ivory Coast. We are so thankful the Lord put this ministry on our hearts and that He is so faithful in providing their needs each month!

After the war began in September of 2002, we came back to the States for a few months until things could cool down a little bit over there in the Ivory Coast. When we got back to Africa, things had drastically changed in our beloved country and most all the missionaries had left the field. I must admit it was not only a lonely time but a scary time as well. We wanted to stay and help the people in any way we could but the Lord had other plans for our lives.

After being up all night with Arnold because of severe chest pains, we transported him down to the capital city, Abidjan, in the back of a van on a mattress. He was immediately put in ICU in the Canadian hospital, although the facilities had really gone down medically and structurally. They wouldn't let me go in ICU to see him. I later found out that there was a woman in the bed right next to him vomiting blood and she soon died with spinal meningitis! After he was transferred to another room, the African doctor told us that Arnold wouldn't be able to leave Africa for a couple of months, but we were desperate to get him out of there and get some good medical help back here in the States.

One day, a male nurse came in the room to check Arnold's IV fluids. He had a metal tray propped on one of his arms and it was full of used syringes and needles. The nurse flipped the tray and all the needles went up in the air. One needle came down and stuck upright in Arnold's chest. I almost went into cardiac arrest myself!

During that time of his hospitalization, I went back up-country to our house in Yamoussoukro in the middle of the Ivory Coast. I needed to sell our belongings in order to get money to pay for his hospital stay. How the Lord blessed me and within three days, I had sold or given away everything in our house!

Arnold and I went to the Southern Baptist guesthouse for a while and then we decided to sneak out of the country without the doctors there knowing it. He wasn't getting any stronger and he desperately needed help. We had a rough flight back to Georgia but we were so thankful to get back on American soil.

## Episode 61

# I Knew You'd Come

I have already written about the years I spent away from my precious mama. After my dad passed on, she continued to live alone for a year or so. One day, she was so frightened when a man came to her back door and tried to get in that she decided to listen to her family and move into a smaller apartment.

I think she had some good years in the apartment with her little poodle. All the family visited her often but she still seemed so lonely. When she knew we were coming, she would stand at the window and watch for us! I have that vision of her at the window etched in my mind forever.

Mama had been having some spells of dizziness. This would often happen when she was baking something in the oven. When she would lean down to get the food out, she often lost her balance. We got her one of those medical alerts that she wore around her neck.

One cold afternoon, Mama went out on the back porch to take the trash out. No one knows exactly what happened but she lost her balance, fell on the floor, and broke her hip. Thank the Lord she was able to push the panic button around her neck and it alerted the company that

183

something was wrong. They began to call family members. Our oldest son, Jason, had gone to work that evening but when he got the message, he went back to Mama's apartment. He rang the front door bell and when she didn't answer he ran to the back porch and found her. Mama said that she saw Jason actually leap over that fence without touching it. He picked her up and took her in the house.

She had to have hip surgery and needed someone to stay at the house with her. My sister stayed six hours a day, I stayed six hours a day and then we hired a lady to come and sit with her for 12 hours during the night. Well, that lasted for two nights. On the second night, the sitter must have been asleep in the living room because Mama somehow scooted down to the edge of the bed and fell off again.

I never told Mama we wouldn't put her in a nursing home but in my heart I always thought that I could never do it. Now we had come to that part of our lives that I had always dreaded. Mama needed around the clock attention. My sister and I went and spoke to the director of the nursing home. The Lord blessed from the very first day. The director showed us a huge bright room which was usually reserved for married couples. We were told that Mama could have that room. What an extra blessing! When we talked to Mama about it, she said one thing. "I know my girls will only do what is best for me!" She was an angel!

The first night in the nursing home was the worst! Till this day, my sister and I can't talk about that night without crying! Mama got a wonderful roommate and they became best friends. My sister and I visited every day. It tickled us to see Mama and Mrs. Lula getting all primped up to go to the bingo game. I walked in one day and Mama was drawing on some dark eyebrows and Mrs. Lula was painting on some bright red lips! I couldn't help but laugh as the two of them took off down the hall, side by side, in their wheelchairs going to play bingo! I knew everything was okay when I called Mama one night to say that I was coming over to visit with her. I had just left her a few hours before! There was silence on the phone. She sweetly told me she had just found out there would be a bingo game that night and she and Mrs. Lula didn't want to miss that. She then proceeded to tell me that I could come on over if I wanted to but I would have to go and play bingo with them. I burst into laughter! I told Mama that I thought I would just stay at home that Friday night and be with the family. She certainly wasn't lonely anymore!

We were thrilled when Mama was asked to be in the pageant to choose Miss Starcrest! My sister and I dolled her up like she was going to the senior prom! She was beautiful that night and how proud we were of her when she won! You could tell by the look on her face that she loved every single minute of it!

Mama was 84 years old. When she became confused one day, all of the family was so upset. I had been at the nursing home earlier that day but had come home to prepare dinner. Some of our children had come over to eat that night. Our middle son, John, came in and told me that he had just left the nursing home and Mama's mind was as clear as could be. I never ate a bite but rushed back over to the nursing home. Mama always went to sleep at eight o'clock as soon as Wheel of Fortune was finished. It was nine-thirty when I got to her room and I thought she would be sound asleep. I gently opened the door and there she was! She was propped up on her side, wide-eyed and this is what she said. "I knew you were coming!" I pulled a chair up to the bed as close as I could get to her. I pulled the curtain so as not to disturb Mrs. Lula. John was right. Mama's mind was as clear as crystal. We talked about days gone by. I asked her so many questions about so many things. Before we knew it, it was midnight! I could hardly believe time had passed so quickly! Before I left, I felt this huge lump in my throat. I asked my mama, "Do you know how much I love you?" We had been holding hands ever since I got there as we talked. Her answer will always be in my thoughts and in my heart. She said, "Honey, some things you don't even have to ask about!" I left crying but thankful for that precious time we had together.

The next day she was so upset. She didn't remember that I had been there. In fact, she asked Arnold why I never came to see her anymore. The Lord gave me that one last time to be able to share my heart and spend those moments together. I will forever be grateful for that!

Several months passed and Mama's health began to fail. Finally, she stopped eating and even drinking. In her last days, we stayed at the nursing home 24 hours a day. Even when she was unconscious, someone was with her every minute! My sister and I had been with Mama all night on that Friday. When our aunts came to the nursing home on Saturday morning, we decided to go home and get a shower. I can remember lying on my bed and the tears and grief just poured out of my being. I was almost screaming, "Lord, take her and please don't let her suffer anymore!" That was the second time in my life that I realized that you can love someone so much that death would be better than watching them lie and suffer day after day. The phone rang. My aunt said that Mama had gone home to be with Jesus! We rushed back to the nursing home. The next three days remain blurry in my mind.

As her friends and family gathered together at the funeral, we sang "What a Day That Will Be." This same song was sung at Daddy's funeral eight years earlier! I have had more than my share of goodbyes in my life. All those years of going back and forth to Africa and having to leave family and friends here and having to say goodbye to our African Christians over there! Will the goodbyes ever end? I am glad I can say with all certainty that one day, yes, one day soon, there won't be any tears to dim the eyes and no more painful separations. So, whatever we go through in this life, we can look back and know that it was worth it all!

## Episode 62

# "Mama Skelton," A Praying Mom

I have just finished telling you the story about my own mama. In reality, I found my second mama, and also a dear and precious friend, when I married into the Skelton family. We were close from the beginning and stayed that way until we were separated by death!

Mama Skelton was one of the best cooks who ever lived! She would always amaze me by having the family dinner on the table at precisely 4 p.m., when Daddy Skelton would walk in the door from his job at Lockheed in Marietta, Georgia.

Before Arnold surrendered to the Lord to preach and go to a foreign mission field, she was in constant prayer for him and always encouraged him to follow Jesus! I will never forget what she told the Lord. She said that she knew Arnold was being called to the mission field so please send him anywhere, but don't send him to Africa! We laughed about that little talk with the Lord for many years!

Mama Skelton came to visit us three different times in Africa. She never got sick at all and loved every minute of her time there. Oh, how the Africans loved and honored her when she came over!

My mama and Mama Skelton became best of friends. She would even leave pajamas, pillows, and toothbrushes at my mama's house because our parents visited each other so often. You don't usually find that closeness in a family!

We had just arrived back in Africa when we got the devastating news that Mama Skelton had been in a terrible car accident. Arnold wasn't able to return home because of finances but she had a wonderful family and friend support team who nursed her back to health.

The news was shocking and heartbreaking several years later when we were here in the States for furlough. She had another car accident and never gained consciousness. Mama Skelton stayed in the hospital for five days before she made her final trip to be with Jesus. I remember the song that was sung at her funeral, "When Answers Aren't Enough, There Is Jesus!" We continue to miss her every day, even after all these many years. She died in 1989 and was only 65 years old! Some things in life we will never understand. One thing we are sure of: the fervent prayers of this praying mother reached the throne of Heaven and we know that because of her example and prayers, the Lord called and used her son in a mighty way to preach the Gospel to those who have never heard before! We will be with my precious mother-in-law again one day and there will never be any more goodbyes!

**Episode 63**

# Ticks, Ticks, Everywhere!

Our life was definitely changing. Ivory Coast was split right down the middle and most all of the other missionaries had already left the country. Arnold and I were getting ready to go back to Africa without any of our five children. We bought a little dog to take with us. We named him Snickers and he looked just like Toto on "The Wizard of Oz" movie. We had always had children with us since our first trip over in June of 1970. Needless to say, I was having an extremely difficult time saying goodbye to our children and grandchildren. Our Africa house had always been the center of gatherings for the missionary children of all ages. What fun we had through the years!

When we arrived in the Ivory Coast, as usual, we had to find an empty house to get it ready for our furniture and for moving in. This particular house we had found needed so much work done on it. We knew it would take several weeks to get it ready. One of the missions there in Yamoussoukro told us that we could stay in their previous school dormitory as long as we liked. I was shocked the day we drove up and went inside. There was a stove, a fridge, a table with benches and some dirty old mattresses. Our container hadn't arrived yet so we had absolutely nothing to use in the dorm. We had to buy some cheap plates, cups, and utensils from the market. We had "roughed it" many times through the years but I was not expecting what happened there in that dormitory.

The first day, Coulibaly came over and helped me scrub the two bathrooms. We threw bleach all over it to disinfect the whole area. After cleaning all day, I was exhausted. This dormitory had been vacant for a couple of years and no one had gone inside to take care of it. Arnold and I put our single mattresses on the floor side by side and thought we would have a decent night of sleep. Wrong! I woke up in the middle of the night and ticks were crawling all over the walls, all over the floors, all over our mattresses and all over us! I shined the flashlight on Arnold and there were several ticks crawling around on him! I had a major panic attack! Where had these awful things come from? Then to make it worse, the next morning there was a huge black spider on my mattress that was squashed in about ten different pieces! Yep! I had rolled over it a few times! We sprayed and sprayed but nothing got rid of those awful ticks!

Another part of the tick saga is that about a week or so later, I had a very high fever and was aching all over. I must have passed out because when I woke up, Coulibaly's wife was sitting on the floor next to my mattress and she was putting cold compresses on my forehead. I went to the doctor and sure enough, and not surprisingly, I had tick fever! It left me as weak as water!

Our poor little Snickers! Every morning, until we left that dormitory several weeks later, I took about an hour to pick ticks off of our little dog. I had a cup of bleach and I would put the live ticks in that until they stopped moving. Until this day, I cringe when I see a tick! What a nightmare!

The first night we slept in our house, we were so relieved and happy to be out of that dormitory. We had our nice bed all set up and Arnold had just said, "Oh, praise the Lord, we have our own clean and tick-free bed. How wonderful to be off the floor!" About ten minutes later, we heard a crack and our bed fell in! We were once again on the floor but with no ticks crawling around. We laughed and laughed! Looking back, experiences like that are special because they help you to appreciate and be more thankful for the easier times! One thing for sure, I hope I never have to share my sleeping quarters with ticks again!

## Episode 64

# Victory Rests With The Lord

As I sit writing on this beautiful island, Man-O-War, Bahamas, my soul is overwhelmed by the goodness and the mercy of our Lord! Arnold is over on the island next to us called Marsh Harbor. Last night he ended a six-day crusade preaching to the Haitians at their church on the island. If you know Arnold very well then you can imagine how thrilled he was to be preaching in French again!

This has indeed been a trying year of tears, death, and sickness. Two of my dearest friends have gone to be with the Lord during the last twelve months. One's death was expected, the other one was not. The very thought of Heaven gets sweeter and more real as the days go by!

In October of this same year, I was rushed to the hospital with the beginning of kidney failure. Earlier that week Arnold and I had gone to the mountains with our oldest son and his family. I felt especially tired and dizzy during our time there but thought I was dehydrated. I almost passed out in a small shop, but after drinking two bottles of water, I felt better.

We came on home and went to our daughter's house in Augusta. By that time, I was almost writhing in pain, even when the grandchildren would barely touch me. Natalie went upstairs and looked online for the cholesterol medications I had been taking for the past two weeks. She came down and said, "Mom, I think you are going into kidney failure." The trip back to Covington was almost unbearable. The next day the room was going round and round and I knew I had to go to the ER immediately. It didn't take the doctors long to find out that I had a life threatening disease called rhabdomyolysis.

The doctors began talking about possible dialysis and it really scared me. To top it all, the kidney specialist came in my room and blurted out that he had found a protein in my urine and he thought I had multiple myeloma or cancer of the blood! He took special blood tests and told us that it would take at least eight days to get the final results. All of our children were devastated! I think those eight days were the longest ones of my life! I am very thankful that the special blood tests came back normal.

The next part of this story is difficult for me to write but very amusing and real, to say the least! I love songs about Heaven! I cry with joy at the thought of being there with all my friends and loved ones who have gone on before. I get happy when I sing the songs, "What a Day That Will Be," "When We All Get to Heaven," etc. BUT when I thought I may be going there in the immediate, I realized how much I love life. I love my husband, children, grandchildren, family and friends! I was feeling like Bob Harrington, the evangelist from New Orleans, who once commented, "I know I am saved and am on my way to Heaven. I just don't want to be on the next load!" Well put, Brother Bob! I am so thankful that I don't have cancer and I am getting stronger every day! But much more than that, I am thankful that when I do cross over to meet my Lord, I will have a home in Heaven prepared for me!

We have no idea as to what the future holds for each of us. Thank the Lord we don't! I need child-like faith in trusting the Lord in every phase of my life. Our own children never once worried about having enough food or clothing when they were growing up. They never wondered what they would do if they got really sick. They knew that their dad and I would be there to take care of them. Why should they have to worry? "Lord, I trust you. Help me to trust you more! Lord, I love you. Help me to love you more!"

Proverbs 21:30 says, "There is no wisdom, no insight, no plan that can succeed against the Lord! The horse is made ready for the day of battle, but victory rests with the Lord."

Whatever happens in the days, months, and years ahead, I know it will be for my good, His glory, and according to His will for my life!

## Episode 65

# Bits and Pieces #1

On the day of my eighth grade graduation into high school, my grandfather passed away after a long bout of prostate cancer. I remember hearing the news while I was at school but I stayed on as we were practicing for the ceremony. When I got home, my dad told me that Mama wouldn't be able to come to the graduation since her dad had just passed away. I was sad but I certainly understood all that was going on.

As we lined up and started our procession into the gymnasium that night, I felt someone tugging on my graduation gown, and there was my precious mama sitting there! All she said was, "Hey honey! I am here!" I will never forget as long as I live how my mama put me first, even though her heart was literally breaking in two that night. She was always such a wonderful example to me in every way! I am a grandmother of ten precious children now but there are times that I still weep for my mama! There are still things I yearn to share with her and unload on her but those days have gone now!

When I see a woman with her elderly mother out in a store or in a doctor's office I always take the opportunity to tell them how blessed they are to still have each other. Good grief! I am bawling as I write these bits and pieces of my life! If any of my readers still have their parents with them, love them, spend much time with them and do all you can with them and for them. Make good memories because memories are all you will have left one day! I will see my mama and dad again in Heaven and the very thought of being reunited with them makes my heart pound with joy! What a day!

## Episode 66

# Bits and Pieces #2

Our youngest son, Grady, was always watching and observing people, especially his own dad. We weren't too surprised when Grady announced at two years old that he wanted to be just like "Daddy" when he went to church. Grady wanted to wear a black suit, walk up and down the aisles greeting people, and wanted to have a big black Bible under his arm. When some friends came over, I asked Grady to share his "dream of being like Daddy" with them. He told them about wearing the dark suit and walking around greeting people, but for some reason he forgot the part about the big black Bible under his arm. When I gently reminded him that he forgot to tell them what he would have under his arm, we all burst into laughter when he thought for a few seconds and in a loud voice answered, "Uh, de-od-uh-wunt!"

## Episode 67

# Bits and Pieces #3

When the children were growing up in the Ivory Coast, we had a special and private area where we would go so that we could swim in the lagoon. The lagoon is a body of water cut off from a larger body by a reef or sand coral. In this case, the lagoon was separated from the Atlantic Ocean. We had so many wonderful days there with inner tubes floating around in the water. There were countless picnics there on the beach!

One day we were all swimming in the lagoon and I sat watching Arnold, Jason, and two more men swim with inner tubes all the way across. I remember saying out loud how very blessed we were to have such a wonderful place to swim and with such privacy! There were two of us families and we had the most relaxing and perfect day together.

The sun began to go down and both families packed up our vehicles to return to our house. As we were pulling away, an African man came running to the car! He stopped us and said, "Thank goodness I caught you in time to warn you not to go near the lagoon today, as a female crocodile had babies and she had already attacked some Africans who were at the edge of the water washing clothes!" Oh, my goodness! I often think of that day and how we had such a wonderful time without a fear of any kind! How the Lord takes care of His own!

Another time, Arnold brought a crocodile to our house in Africa. He put it in our outside storage room. He wanted to make a pet out of it! Are you kidding me? Who would want a dangerous crocodile as a pet? Arnold would open the storage room door and poke it with a broom! It would make a horrible hissing sound! Oh, dear, what big teeth it had! I insisted that Arnold make a choice. Me or the crocodile!

Years later, John, our middle son, followed in his dad's footsteps and decided that he wanted to keep three baby crocodiles in our back yard! It was okay until they began to grow! After much insistence from me, John reluctantly put them back in the lake in front of our house. Although some of the African pets were dangerous, I am thankful that our children got to experience the excitement and wonder of living in a different culture and country.

## Episode 68

# Bits and Pieces #4

Arnold had been in Abidjan for a few days and was supposedly on his way home. As it got later and later, I realized that something must be wrong. About that time, Arnold drove up the driveway and I will never forget the sight I saw as long as I live. He was covered in blood from his head all the way down to his feet. I almost fainted when he got out of the truck. He immediately stripped himself of all his clothes and we burned everything he had on within minutes.

He had been on his way home and saw that a huge bus had been in a terrible accident. As usual, he had stopped to try and do anything he could to help. There were dead people all over the sides of the road. Arnold saw an old white-haired man moaning and crying on the ground. The man was mangled almost to death and completely covered with oozing blood. He reached up toward Arnold with his arms and was begging for someone to help him. Arnold gently picked this old man up in his arms and cradled him like a baby until he took his last breath!

If Arnold would risk his own health by cradling a stranger who was dying in his arms, how much more does he love the very people he has given his life for, gone to live with, won to the Lord, and taught them the Word? I may be a little bit prejudiced but it sounds like real love to me!

## Episode 69

# How Could This Be Happening?

On a warm summer night, I had grilled a steak for dinner and had just put it on the table with a salad and fries. Arnold sat down at the table but told me he didn't feel good at all. When I pressed him on what that meant, he said he just felt "funny." I suggested that he lie down for a few minutes and I would leave the food on the table for when he felt like eating. He agreed!

I went on over to our youngest daughter's house to visit with her for a while. I don't remember how long I stayed but it had just turned dark when I came back to our house. There was only one light on and it was in our bedroom. I came in and shouted out my usual, "I'm home!" There was no response at all! I followed the light and saw that Arnold's jacket, the coat rack, and the telephone were lying on the floor. What had happened?

That is when I saw Arnold sitting up against the closet wall in a fetal position. His hands were shaking as if he was having a seizure. I walked over to him and asked the most stupid thing. "You wouldn't tease me like this, would you?" I lifted his chin and I saw blood coming out of his mouth. That is when I knew he was in real trouble!

I called 911 and also my next door neighbor. The neighbor was at my door before I could get it unlocked! He held Arnold in his arms until the paramedics arrived. The paramedics cut off Arnold's clothes and that is when I realized that Arnold hadn't made one sound since I found him in the closet. His eyes were open but were fixed and staring up to the ceiling. Jason, our oldest son, and I were following the speeding ambulance and saw it pull over to a parking lot. Arnold was having severe seizures and the paramedics had called for the firemen to come back and help with him. Jason climbed up in the ambulance and with all of his strength, helped hold his dad down on the stretcher.

When we finally arrived at the hospital, Arnold uttered one single word during all this time. He cried out, "Jesus!" The next few minutes were spent putting in a breathing tube as he wasn't able to breathe on his own. He was taken to ICU and carefully monitored all night. The next morning Arnold was sent to Emory University Hospital by a medical helicopter. Things were getting worse and worse!

On Sunday morning, the third day of this unbelievable nightmare, the doctors told us that Arnold's organs were beginning to shut down, one by one. His kidneys and lungs were not functioning on their own. We couldn't believe our ears! What had caused all of this? All we knew was that he had his third heart attack during this ordeal. Jason looked around at me and asked, "Do you want me to call the Africans?" I said to go ahead and call them so that they could pray for their spiritual Papa! I later heard that they got as many of our Christians together as possible in Africa and were all praying together and begging the Lord to spare Arnold's life!

On the third day, the doctors thought Arnold wouldn't make it through the night. The nurses were told to let anyone in to see him that came by. There was little hope that Arnold would survive.

Sometime during the next day, things began to change. Arnold was still on a respirator and unconscious but his organs were beginning to respond to the treatment and the prayers. Nevertheless, he remained in this condition for eleven days before they tried to remove the respirator!

I remember one night during this horrible ordeal that I had an excruciating and painful earache in the middle of the night. I was walking the floor in front of ICU and I could hear each pump and swish of air from Arnold's ventilator. Guess I was having my own pity party that night because these are my exact thoughts. "Here I am with a terrible earache and the only person in all the world who cares about my earache and would be taking care of me is laying in there with a ventilator breathing for him!"

I didn't sleep any all night long just knowing that the doctors would be removing the respirator the next morning. All our children were gathered outside the ICU doors anxious to see what would happen. Would their dad be able to breathe on his own? Would he ever be like he was before all of this happened? So many questions! I love the song, "When answers aren't enough, there is Jesus!"

It took a while but Arnold was indeed able to breathe on his own and they removed the ventilator! What an unforgettable day! Later on, Arnold was inside a tiny ICU room and the door was closed going out to the other nurses' desks. I heard him screaming out and when I approached his bed, this is what he said in a low and calm voice. "I know what I want! I am so thirsty. Please get me something to drink." He drank two cups of apple juice and two cups of water without stopping for a breath. He then closed his eyes and whispered, "Thank you! That is all I wanted!" He slept for the rest of the day.

Three days later, Arnold was released from Emory University Hospital. Taking care of him at home was difficult to say the least. His body would jerk so violently at night that I would have to put my legs and arms around him just to hold him on the bed. He would perspire so badly that I would have to change the sheets twice during the night. As time passed, he began to sleep normally again and that was a wonderful blessing for both of us!

We don't know why this happened and what caused this to happen. Was it a seizure that caused him to have his third heart attack or was it the heart attack that caused him to have a seizure? Whatever happened, the Lord's eyes were on us and we will forever be thankful to Him for His mercy, love, and protection in our lives. All praise goes to Him!

## Episode 70

# The Struggling Sardine

I am often reminded of our trip with my parents to Jacksonville Beach, Florida. As we walked on the fishing pier, I saw a small sardine lying on the wooden planks, gasping. My daddy reached down, picked it up, and threw it out into the waves. It was a pitiful sight as the ocean kept tossing it back and forth. Being already exhausted and half-dead, the small sardine simply rode with the waves until its strength returned and it was able to continue into the rolling ocean – free and safe at last!

I thought of my own life. Sometimes I have gotten so dry and entangled in the worries and cares of this life that I begin to wonder if I will ever really get the victory by completely trusting in Jesus for my concerns. At that moment, when I feel that I can't continue any longer, my Heavenly Father reaches down and picks me up, and I find complete and perfect peace as waves of love encompass me. I am safe – yes, safe and secure at last in my Father's everlasting arms!

Jesus never takes His eyes off me as I gasp for air. He knows how much I can and will endure. He is there all the time! Lord, help me to trust you and rest in your perfect care in the difficult and trying times, as well as, in the good, easy times.

**Episode 71**

# Only One Life

When I was a Brownie Scout, the fad was to own an autograph book and have all your friends sign it. One old fogey, about thirty years old (well, it was old to me since I was twelve at the time), asked to sign my autograph book. After writing a few lines, she folded down the page and gave it back to me. A few days later I was reading through my book. All my friends had written really cute things like, "U R 2 sweet 2 B 4 gotten" or "Roses are red, violets are blue, my feet stink and so do you," etc. Then I came to the folded page. The words she wrote literally changed my life. "Only one life, will soon be past. Only what is done for Christ will last." I had been saved for a year and didn't fully understand the meaning of those words at that time. Now I do!

Arnold and I feel such an urgency to get the Gospel to lost Africans. There's not much time left to work for Jesus. Our prayer is that the Lord would burden us, and you reading this book, to take our eyes off material things and keep our eyes on Heavenly things that have eternal value. John 9:4 tells us, "I must work the works of Him that sent me, while it is day: the night cometh, when no man can work."

After 35 years of serving Jesus in Africa, I can say from experience that the Lord has truly kept His promises to us. His divine presence has sustained us and has gone before us in every situation. How I praise Him for calling us to serve Him in the Ivory Coast of West Africa! Arnold and I will never regret for a single minute that we have spent the best part of our lives in serving Him, according to His will, and His calling.

# Conclusion and Beginning

Arnold and I wrote a book several years ago. The purpose was to write down our life's journey to be able to share with our children, grandchildren, and great grandchildren as the years pass on! Since we were still ministering in Africa, we had 1,000 copies printed here in the States but then returned to Africa. The copies sold within a few months!

Since that time, so much more has happened and a lot of changes have taken place in our ministry. This book has been burning in my heart for a long time, so I am ever so thankful that it is finally complete and we can share our story with others!

Years before war broke out in the Ivory Coast, the Lord had already placed a burden on our hearts for orphans and widows who had no place to live and barely enough food to eat on a daily basis. We were already asking for clothes, toys, and other items to begin an orphanage when the country was suddenly divided in half because of a civil war.

We had come home for a couple of months but then returned to Africa right in the middle of the war. In 2004, Arnold had his second heart attack there in the Ivory Coast. We had come back to get medical help and that is when the doctors told us we could not go back to the Ivory Coast, as Arnold's heart was too weak and it would probably kill him. This news was devastating to us! We had already served in Africa for 35 years and our hopes were to continue on. Our plans aren't always God's plans!

The burden to have an orphanage and take care of those poor precious orphans resurfaced in such a strong way and we realized this was His plan for our lives at this time.

Since we came back from Africa, we have had 34 orphans living in a rented church building and sleeping all over the floor! Our hearts are so burdened for them and we are praying that the proceeds of this book will help to complete the orphanage so that they can have a roof over their heads and beds to sleep on.

How blessed we are to have Coulibaly and his precious wife, Elisabeth, taking care of and loving these orphans twenty-four hours a day! In one of our episodes, I told all about Coulibaly and how he is an orphan himself. What better person to head up an orphanage than one who understands how it is to have no one to love and take care of them as a child. Every month when we send money over to the orphanage, Coulibaly takes photos of whatever he purchased and then sends us receipts from the store where he bought the needed items. That is real accountability!

Coulibaly got saved through Arnold's preaching when he was only seventeen years old. He claims us as his real mom and dad and we do the same to him and his family!

My heart's desire is that you, our readers, will better understand our lives and ministry throughout all these years! I pray that hearts will be touched and that our Lord will be glorified for truly, "Great things He has done!"

Arnold and preacher friends unloading equipment
before evangelistic service.

Arnold in the midst of those attending a week-long
Bible Camp.

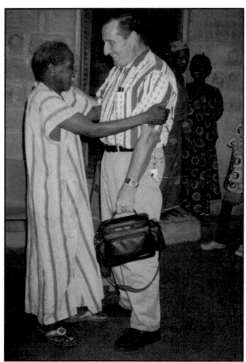

Arnold being welcomed back by a 90-year-old elder of the village church.

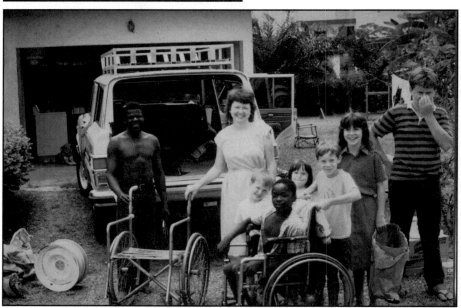

Linda with our five children and Matthias
(See Episode 35).

Arnold baptizing
new convert.
Notice two
crocodiles
looking on.
Curious
or Hungry?

Linda standing
with Boto
and his family
The little boy in
Boto's arms is
the son who had
his throat slit.
(See
Episode 52).

Our Yamoussoukro orphans with Coulibaly and his wife,
Elisabeth, directors of the orphanage.

Work on the septic system for the new orphanage compound is all manual labor.

Orphanage Main Dormitory.
Approximately 40 orphans and widows will live here.
Work continues as this book goes to print.
Proceeds from book sales will be used
to finish this section.

# Facts about the Ivory Coast and the Gospel Baptist Mission:

- Gospel Baptist Mission of Ivory Coast (M.B.E.) "Mission Baptist Evangelique" was established with the Minister of the Interior of Ivory Coast in 1973.

- M.B.E. has over 60 churches.

- National Bible Institute has six professors and is totally run and directed by nationals. We use three months theory, three months practice, three months theory, three months practice method for training our preachers for three years before they can be brought before the Presbytery for examination and approval for ordination. All financial support is by faith, in whatever the churches they serve, offers them in love. There are no set salaries for any preachers. There are set salaries for teachers in our four schools.

- One central orphanage, in the village of Tiebissou, with four war widows helping with the children and 34 orphans as of this year, 2015.

- Five circuits of churches in four regions of the Ivory Coast.

- We have 17 ordained preachers for the five circuits of churches.

- The population of the Ivory Coast is: 24,976,000 people and 66 tribal groups and languages. French is the national language of the country.

- 16% of population is Roman Catholic

- 4% of population is Evangelical Christian

- 67% of population is animists (spirit worshippers, idols, gods of wood, stone, metals, masks, etc.)

- 13% of population is animist mixtures and false religions

For further information, please contact:

**_Arnold and Linda Skelton_**
770-639-7671 (cell)
770-385-0167 (home)
larci35@yahoo.com

Our mission agency:

Central Missionary Clearinghouse
P.O. BOX 219228
Houston, Texas 77218
Telephone: 1-800-262-7729